DWAYNE WALKER

Create or Die

48 keys of Creativity

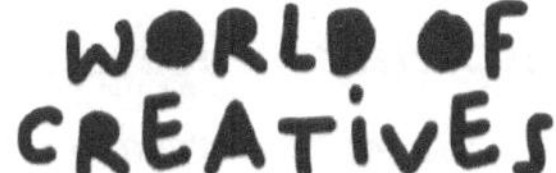

Ife Walker, thank you for encouraging me to express myself in this way. Many of the topics nestled in these chapters were inspired by our conversations. Thank you for being my muse, my confidant, and my unwavering supporter.

Love, Dwayne Walker

If this book inspires you, do something creative with the book cover and share it with me. Feel free to paint on it, write a story or a poem on it, or you can even film a video or make music with it. I'm looking forward to seeing what you create.

DWAYNE WALKER, CREATE OR DIE

Contents

Preface

Most people see the words "Create or Die," and they think I am talking about a physical death—but you, you see the world differently than most. Something in you knew that I am talking about an abstract death. For people like me and you, we feel alive when we create, and death are all the things that pull us away from our passions and self-expressions. It's the schools. It's the jobs. It's the systems. It's the rules. It's the norms. It's the insecurities. It's the doubt. It's all the chains that keep us grounded when all we want to do is fly. Our purpose on this planet, in this short span of time we have to experience it, is to bring our ideas to life. We live to create. Do you want the keys to unlocking the chains holding you back from your creative potential?

Magic Key

REAL MAGIC

…And now, for my next trick, I need an unsuspecting reader.

Ahh, you! Yes, you…

Hold your hand out, palm up, as if you're preparing to catch a falling leaf. Visualize in your mind an object, say a book, that doesn't exist, never before seen. Think of an idea for its title, the design of its cover, its genre, its theme, and even its thickness. Feel its weight in the palm of your hand. Now, with a deep breath, close your eyes and imagine that book materializing, then on the count of three, open your eyes slowly.

One…two…three—Imagine how magical it would've felt if when you opened your eyes the book you visualized was resting in your hand.

Well, my friend, that's exactly how I created this book.

A few years ago, I was struck by an idea for a book that would unveil the extraordinary power of creativity. Like a deep breath, I inhaled countless research studies, biographies, and interviews, absorbing each as a source of inspiration. Then, I exhaled my own findings, perspectives, and insights, condensing them into these pages. That's how this book, once a mere figment of imagination, came to life.

Like magic, I created something out of nothing, bridging the gap between ideas and reality. In alternative cases, this magic happens instantaneously, like during the spontaneous composition of jazz music or improv poetry. Other times, it can take years to materialize, like fulfilling the vision of a classic film or technological innovation.

Regardless of the complexities of an idea, there's a special key required to unlock the power to bring it to life.

The key is called creativity.

You see, creativity unlocks many magical doors.

Creativity unlocks the way you think. Your mind opens up to differing viewpoints. You approach challenges with ease, becoming bolder as you embrace failure. You observe the world like a baby with curious eyes, finding joy and beauty in the little things. This leads to a more intentional engagement with the world, enriching your life in the process.

Most importantly, creativity unlocks the pursuit of a deeper understanding of oneself. The act of being creative is a mindful act that can improve your mental health, reduce stress, and boost your mood. You may find that you are more vulnerable with yourself. Creativity is an instinctual natural therapy that will help you process and cope with the roller coaster of life.

Like the trick I performed at the beginning of this chapter, creativity unlocks your potential to transform your ideas into tangible realities. As mystical as that sounds, the real magic happens when you share your creations with the world. Through creative works like literature, film, music, food, business, dance, and art, everyone can share their narrative, fostering global empathy. What starts as an expression of individuality can often make a social impact, influencing pop culture, trends, and societal norms. This key harnesses the potential to change the world for generations to come.

THE CATALYST

We tend to idolize a very particular type of human. We fill stadiums to sing their songs in unison. We wear their clothes to gain confidence. We fly across the world to gather in a quiet room around a blank wall to stare attentively at their brush strokes. We host worldwide competitions to witness them break records. We build habits around their technology because it makes our daily lives easier.

We admire them so much that we call them legends as if they're Greek gods. They seem like heroes who possess superhuman abilities. And it's true. They are superhuman, but they're not beyond human. Instead, they all have one thing in common. They all hold the key. They use it to unlock a source deep within their humanity and use it to influence the world.

This source possesses great power, yet it doesn't limit itself to only a small, particular group of people. It's the most abundant natural resource available to humanity. It's everywhere, freely flowing through everyone, yearning for people to tap into it. The world is filled with superhumans who are unaware of their superpowers. Chances are, you're one of them.

But don't worry. This moment is a crucial part of your heroic journey. This book you're reading is the catalyst to unlocking your powers.

It's going to show you that creativity is not what you think. It's more. It's transformative, it's empowering, and it's one of the most valuable gifts you will ever give yourself.

NOTES ON CREATIVITY

I structured this book similar to how most creators think, thoughts seemingly scattered and random, but all connecting. It is not written like a long, drawn-out lecture. Instead, each key is packed with short bursts of interesting, interconnected information, studies, and commentary that converge into profound insights.

Over the last few years I've dissected the lives of history's most creative geniuses, read countless research studies on creativity's effect on humans, and practiced the things I've learned in my everyday life. The pages in this book are all of my private notes on creativity packaged into a collection of 48 keys. They're filled with facts and historical accounts, but I also share my opinions, ideas, and theories. It's a blend of fact and fiction, reality and imagination, science and art. My journey of researching creativity revealed unexpected truths. If you keep an open mind, my only goal is to teach you the lessons I learned from years of researching creativity.

With each key, you'll learn about a creative genius, gain a new perspective, a fresh insight, and a powerful tool that empowers you to innovate, inspire, and leave a mark on this world. Use these keys to become a more impactful creator while embarking on a profound voyage of self-discovery, elevating your artistry, your ventures, and your life.

These pages hold the answers to unlocking your creative potential. It's the elixir of life for your creative soul. Brace yourself for a journey that will change how you perceive yourself, the world, and the boundless realm of creativity. By the end of this book, you will be more able to tap into the endless flow of inspiration at will, think of innovative ideas, develop strategies to execute your ideas, and, in doing so, live a more fulfilling life while inspiring others. I wrote *Create or Die: 48 Keys of Creativity* for people like me, creative thinkers who have a dying urge to create something great in this world. Maybe you have ideas for hit songs, art shows, movie scripts, YouTube channels, clothing lines, performances, books, apps, or businesses. If you have a dying urge to create something impactful like history's greatest creative minds, you're in the right place. Even if only a tiny part of you identifies as an artist, performer, videographer, writer, musician, chef, athlete, influencer, developer, builder, entrepreneur, or any other type of creator, take this key. Read this book. Embrace your catalyst. Unlock your creative potential. It will change your life and, if you wish, it will give you the power to change the world.

Key of Humanity

"The urge to destroy is also a creative urge!"—Pablo Picasso

THE FUNDAMENTALS

Creativity is fundamental to being human. Our brains are wired to create. Our imagination feeds our curiosity, driving us to invent, design, improve and create. It is at the essence of who we are. A major part of our humanity that stands out from other organisms comes from the fraction of our DNA that fuels our creativity. That's where the magic happens; our complex language, our artistic expressions, our architectural marvels, our scientific discoveries, our shared beliefs and values, our medical breakthroughs, our technological advancements. Strip each of those away and we're left naked in a world where the 2% genetic separation between humans and chimps would blur into obscurity.[1]

We celebrate this beauty in people like Beyoncé, Elon Musk, Kobe Bryant, and Albert Einstein, who are famous for their jaw-dropping creative feats. This norm makes most people believe that creativity is limited to proclaimed geniuses. That's a myth. Creativity is

---

[1] Csikszentmihalyi, M. (2015). Creativity: The psychology of discovery and invention. Harper Perennial Modern Classics.

not exclusive to any single person. Visionary thinking isn't tied to your skills, status, location, gender, race, or age. Having a powerful imagination is innate. We just have to choose to embrace it.

IMAGINATION

Oliver Sacks pioneered research on how creative connections are made in the brain. He spent his life learning "how the theater of the mind can be generated by the machinery of the brain."[2] He discovered human brains are wired for imagination by tracking his patients.

Oliver encountered a mysterious mental phenomenon. His patients were blind, yet they were still able to see visual hallucinations. Somehow, they saw things using their mind even though they couldn't see from their eyes.

He tracked his patient's brain activity during their hallucinations. This led to exciting discoveries about how imagination works. When they hallucinated simple shapes, the part of the brain that recognizes patterns lit up. Another brain area responsible for remembering faces activated when they hallucinated people. When the area responsible for eyes and teeth activated, the hallucinations showed deformed people. Another area triggered hallucinations of buildings and landscapes. Another area lit up when they saw cartoons.[3]

Oliver Sacks liked to say we see with our eyes, but we also see with our brains. Imagination is when we see with our brains. The human brain constantly fires off images in our heads regardless of what's right

---

2 in Neuroscience | August 16th, 2016 Leave a Comment. (n.d.). Oliver Sacks explains the biology of hallucinations: "we see with the eyes, but with the brain as well." Open Culture. https://www.openculture.com/2016/08/oliver-sacks-explains-the-biolog y-of-hallucinations.html

3 Sacks, Oliver. 2009. "What Hallucination Reveals about Our Minds." TED. https://w ww.ted.com/talks/oliver_sacks_what_hallucination_reveals_about_our_minds,

in front of our eyes. That's the visionary power of our natural human brain. It's wired to imagine worlds. This is the starting point of every creative journey, an idea so vivid our brain processes and perceives it indistinguishable from reality.

CONNECTEDNESS

Our innate ability to shift between "what exists" and "what could exist" exponentially advanced the human race. This caliber of creativity separates us from other species. Our ancestors collaborated to tackle problems life threw at us. We evaded predators, tamed fire, passed down storytelling, crafted tools, and created vaccines.

Mark Twain said, "There are no original ideas." Nearly a century later, Oliver Sacks' research also defined human creativity as people imitating the world around them. His stance was that we filter those imitations through various mental models and layers. Over time, the images, experiences, and inspirations we absorbed sink into our subconscious. Then long after we've forgotten the source of our inspiration, we use them to imagine new possibilities. Most of our ideas come from these forgotten sparks, inspiring connections stowed deep in our mind and faded by time.

Creativity works within us from a deep subconscious, yet universal, place. We pull our creativity from human's interconnection of ideas, experiences, and imagination. As we evolved, our ability to create evolved too. The energy flowing from one human's creativity to another, generation after generation, gives us an endless supply of new ideas and thoughts. Each creation became a contribution to a chain of brilliance. For example, Albert Einstein would've never been "Einstein" if it wasn't for the collaborative ingenuity of the scientists that came before him. Elon Musk idolized Nikola Tesla, Kobe Bryant's style was influenced by Michael Jordan, and Beyoncé has cited artists like Michael Jackson, Diana Ross, and Aretha Franklin as her inspiration. It's our duty as creatives to contribute to this timeless creative ecosystem daily. Embrace new information. Share ideas. Create.

AN EVOLUTIONARY BOND

In National Geographic's article titled "How Creativity Drives Human Evolution" Simon Worrall interviewed Augustín Fuentes, the author of *The Creative Spark: How Imagination Made Humans Exceptional.* They explored the historical ties between humanity and creativity. A segment from the interview summed it up sweetly saying, "Is creating art a basic evolutionary trait? It depends on what we call 'art.' We tend to think of these beautiful cave paintings of the big mastodons and wild oryx as art. But that's only about 40,000 years old. We know that 85,000 years ago, in southern Africa, our ancestors were carving on ostrich eggshells. Twenty thousand years earlier than that, they were drilling holes in small shells and wearing them around their necks. One hundred thousand years before that, they were crumbling ochre and rubbing it on their bodies. Five hundred thousand years before that, half a million years ago, they were making tools that were incredibly beautiful and more symmetrical and aesthetic than they had to be to do their jobs. Art is deeply integrated in human history."[4]

The more we comb through our history, the more we find art, crafts, dance, music, and stories. Humans and creativity have an unbreakable evolutionary bond. We can't escape it. We should embrace it in its myriad of forms.

---

[4] Worrall, Simon. 2017. "How Creativity Drives Human Evolution." National Geographic. April 23, 2017. https://www.nationalgeographic.com/culture/article/creative-spark-augustin-fuentes-evolution.

DUALITY

One of creativity's most remarkable qualities is its most frightening. It propels the advancement of anything it attaches itself to. Creativity is the root of the ideologies behind both charity and wars. Our ingenuity sent us to outer space yet damaged our planet's ecosystem. We invented life jackets and atomic bombs. Love, hate, joy, pain, and every emotion in between uncontrollably feeds our creativity. Creativity is a duality seeking to both create and destroy. Pablo Picasso said it perfectly: "The urge to destroy is also a creative urge!".

EVERYONE IS CREATIVE

We tend to categorize each other as artistic or non-artistic, creative or uncreative. We follow up these judgments with norms and expectations that influence our behavior. We build imaginary boxes that people willingly fall into. We don't expect non-artists to be creative. There's a sense of mystery behind everyone's creative processes. It's time to lift the veil and reveal the truth. We are all creative beings with the innate ability to turn anything we see and do into a creative endeavor. And if you have forgotten this part of yourself, or didn't know it existed, now is the time to reactivate it. You can create anything from everything. This power is within you whether you choose to unlock it or not.

Liberate yourself. Embrace our shared heritage. Demolish the false barriers between the 'creative' and the 'uncreative,' revealing a fundamental part of the human experience. Creativity is endless, and every step you take into it is a testament to the boundless potential that resides within you.

When you have an idea in your head for a business you want to start, artwork you wish to paint, or song you want to write, you hold the power of answering one question, "Do I want this idea to exist, or not?". The first step to creative genius is acknowledging that being creative is hardwired within you. The profound truth is this: To be human is to be creative.

Key of Inquisition

"Let your voice be heard. Don't stand idly by and let things happen to you. Question everything; be informed."—Madeline Brewer

THE ELEPHANT WHO LOST HIS IDENTITY

Captive elephants don't know their own strength. When they're young, their owner wraps a chain around their leg and connects it to a tree. The young elephant proceeds to try its hardest to detach from the chain, but fails over and over again. Eventually, they give up.

As the elephant grows older, larger, and stronger, they continue to believe the chain around their ankle is their limited physical boundary. The idea becomes so ingrained in their belief system that even when their owners chain them to a small plank of wood they don't try to break free, even though they easily could.

The elephant is completely unaware of their own potential. They don't know the power they truly hold. Just as the captive elephant operates on a foundation of lies, chances are, you are too.

RAISED IN CHAINS

Richard Wurman, the TED Talk founder, suggests, "In school, we're rewarded for having the answer, not for asking a good question." We don't teach kids methods of how to think about the world around them. Instead, kids accept what they learn from their parents, environment, and emotional responses as factual learnings. As they grow older and life fills with complexity, they rely on these 'factual' learnings for understanding. This influences them to transform their learnings into permanent ideas, biases, prejudices, and practices. Unfortunately, most people go their whole lifetime without successfully escaping these frameworks. The key to unlocking these chains is learning how to ask the right questions.

SHOULD YOU TRUST MASS JUDGMENT?

Imagine this scenario: One hundred witnesses are asked to point out a robber from several suspects in a police lineup. Would you agree that the case is closed if all one hundred witnesses select the same suspect? If your answer is "Yes," I'm sorry to break it to you, but you would most likely be wrong. Statistics prove there's a higher chance that the selected person is innocent. As the group of unanimously-agreeing witnesses increases, the probability of them being correct decreases until it is no more valid than a random guess. This phenomenon is the paradox of unanimity.[5]

The Bayesian analysis is the mathematical reasoning behind this paradox. To understand the Bayesian analysis, let's look at flipping

---

[5] Post, David. 2016. "Opinion | the Paradox of Unanimity." Washington Post, February 8, 2016. https://www.washingtonpost.com/news/volokh-conspiracy/wp/2016/02/08/the-paradox-of-unanimity/.

a coin. When you flip a coin, you know it has about a 50% chance to land on either heads or tails. But imagine if you flip the coin one hundred times, and it lands on heads every time. You'd instantly know that something is wrong. Similarly, getting a large group of witnesses to unanimously vote on one robber is so unlikely, according to the laws of probability, it's more likely that something went wrong.

To understand how the paradox relates to your journey of questioning everything, let's explore how it applies to society. Does it mean we should discredit every popular opinion? Not exactly. For simple, easy-to-understand questions, it makes sense for humans to unanimously choose the correct answer. For example, suppose the witnesses had to pick a strawberry out of a lineup of blueberries. In that case, the ease of this task makes the unanimous decision more reliable. But as the complexity of the question increases, the mass consensus becomes more unreliable.

The key here is understanding that the paradox doesn't strictly apply to complete unanimity. A unanimous vote is rare, while a majority vote is common. This paradox applies to both cases because the effect increases as the group consensus increases. Widespread consensus touches a large part of society, including politics, entertainment, business, and religion. When asking yourself tough questions, don't simply fall in line with the majority. Go out and seek answers for yourself first. The more complex the question, the more uncertain society is. The more uncertain a group of people are, the more varied their opinions should be. When faced with a mass-adopted view, research and question it yourself first. There's a high probability the majority doesn't even know they're wrong.

WHAT DOES IT MEAN TO BE OPEN-MINDED?

The definition of reality is the state of things as they actually exist, instead of an idealistic view of them. On the other hand, perception is how we use our senses and mind to focus on, process, recall, explain, comprehend, make decisions about, and act on reality. Perceiving is something you do throughout your life. Eventually, your perceptions become the only baseline you have to define reality.

The problem is that the lens you used to craft your perception is warped. Genetics, experiences, prior knowledge, emotions, sensual limitations, geographical location, preconceived notions, social constructs, social groups, economic classes, cognitive distortions, and self-interest can cloud your perceptions. There's a high chance that what you perceive is reality is merely a limited twisted perception of reality.

Open-mindedness means continuously acknowledging that your reality is your perception, and there is a possibility that your perception skews reality. Open-minded people do two things. First, they accept that other people's perception-based reality is just as acceptable as their own. They respect all points of views because each view is just someone's unique perception. Secondly, they embark on a life-long journey of breaking free from their own perceptions in pursuit of objective reality. This is the path creative geniuses take to ultimate freedom. They open their mind, shift their reality, and look at the world through multiple lenses.

THE DEVIL'S ADVOCATE

Questioning reality from multiple perspectives is essential to fueling and fostering our creative impulse. One way of practicing this is by improving the quality of your conversations with yourself. Approach it like an internal debate. Pretend to be two people holding opposing beliefs. Engage in discussion with each version of yourself, hoping to learn rather than win. Naturally, this process only works when you avoid logical fallacies and personal attacks, and when the nature of the conversation is one of mutual respect. Master these conversations with yourself.

Do not be content exploring your ideas without considering the value of the opposing view. Arguing from both sides can give you more profound and honest insights.

Playing the Devil's advocate is a way of thinking but also a way of doing. A whole new world opens up when you let go of possessing your creative ideas. Approach your creative endeavors in the spirit of the complete opposite. Black becomes white. Bass notes become treble notes. The protagonist becomes the antagonist. Practice using inversion to embrace a deeper sense of beauty and wonder.

WHO? WHAT? WHEN? WHERE? WHY?

When you question everything, you're seeking a better understanding of everything. After you strip away all the fancy words and abstract insights, the core principle of philosophy is to question everything. My high school Language Arts teacher shared a joke that stuck within me: "Who is the greatest philosopher? A four-year-old—all they do all day is ask, 'Why?'"

Questions come in all shapes and sizes. We ask some questions even though we don't have enough information to answer them yet. What is the cure for cancer? How do we reverse aging? There are abstract questions with an infinite number of abstract answers. What is the meaning of life? Why are we here? We may never know the answers to some questions, even though they once had answers. What colors were dinosaurs? We have many theories and guesses based on things we know, but we may never have enough proof to verify. Also, we ignorantly think we have answers to some questions when we don't know we're wrong. For example, society pushed the food pyramid as a science-backed guide to answer the foundational questions surrounding healthy eating. In recent years, more and more research revealed that the USDA pyramid was grossly flawed.[6] Year after year, industries like physics, math, medicine, and psychology make ground-breaking discoveries that shatter what we once believed to be accurate.

Yes, there are things we know, but there's an exponential amount more that we don't know. The purpose of asking questions isn't to always find answers. You often find yourself riddled with more questions after getting your original question answered. Answers beg for more questions. In an interview about government intelligence, Donald Rumsfeld once said, "There are things that we know we know. We also know there are known unknowns. That is to say, we know there's some things we do not know. But there's also unknown unknowns. The ones we don't know we don't know."

By fostering a habit of questioning everything—from your daily choices to the broader beliefs and norms imposed by society—you plant the seed of new possibilities. Through the lens of inquisitiveness and skepticism you move from a passive acceptance of life's routines to an active engagement with the world.

The more questions you ask, the more you gain understanding. As the amount of questions you ask expands, your mind, your life, and the ideas you create will follow suit.

---

6   Willett, Walter C., and Meir J. Stampfer. 2006. "Rebuilding the Food Pyramid." Scientific American 16 (4). https://www.scientificamerican.com/article/rebuilding-the-food-pyramid/.

Key of Experience

"Information is not knowledge. The only source of knowledge is experience."—Albert Einstein

HUNTER S. THOMPSON

Hunter S. Thompson is a journalist who rose from humble beginnings to write arguably the most astonishing discourses on culture and politics. His body of work solidified him as a true iconoclast of his time and a legendary writer. He's hailed as the father of gonzo journalism, a deeply personal reporting style. This new style of journalism rubbed people the wrong way. Hunter explored the uncomfortable facets of American culture and exposed harsh truths of the human condition with bravery and depth.

His style smashed all notions of objective journalism. While every other journalist of his time reported their news from a safe distance, he placed himself at the center of the experience, mixing opinion with fact. He believed gonzo journalism was a much more honest and appropriate way to communicate. One of his most famous demonstrations of this style happened in the 1960's when he spent a year living with the Hells Angels biker gang to write a first-hand account of their lifestyle. He masterfully blended facts with vivid imagery, symbolism, and metaphors to reel the readers into a world where they could see and feel what it was like to be a member of the gang. Since his time, gonzo journalism has become ubiquitous.

His creative philosophy was that journalism is an art where the artist and audience participate in a shared experience. To accomplish this, he expanded his mind by opening up his world. Experiencing the world, rather than just passively observing it, was something Hunter both preached and practiced. He taught us, "Every man is the sum total of his reactions to experiences. As your experiences differ and multiply, you become a different man, and hence your perspective changes. This goes on and on. Every reaction is a learning process; every significant experience alters your perspective."

EPISTEMIC HUMILITY

Epistemic humility is the key to unlocking the mindset needed to expand your mind. The term "epistemic" refers to everything related to knowledge. As human beings, we need to be aware of our epistemic limitations. Having epistemic humility is remaining humble about everything you believe and know. It's accepting that you don't know a lot of things.

Being humble isn't implying you're uneducated. It's accepting that you have limited knowledge of the world and, as a result, there's no limit to your pursuit of knowledge.

No matter how hard you try, you will only know a thin slice of the sum total of knowledge. This could sound depressing, but it should fill you with wonder. Think about it. Isn't it wonderful that there will always be a new creative path to explore, no matter how deep you create? With epistemic humility, every day is a new adventure ripe with possibilities. It reminds us that life has endless surprises around each corner if we open ourselves to it.

This means your potential is limitless. Given enough time, effort, and access to the right resources, you can become whoever you aspire to be. But it also means that there's always the possibility that you're missing a crucial puzzle piece—something you may or may not find out later in life.

The concept of epistemic humility is a reminder that it's alright not to know everything. You can accept your ignorance without feeling smaller. Recognizing your ignorance is the first step toward learning more because if you assume you know everything, you'll never pursue anything.

Limited minds create limited things, so free yourself from what you think you know. Develop into a lifelong learner that's multi-directional and multi-developmental. Learn to look at ideas and problems from above, ahead, beyond, sideways, below, behind, within, and through. Remember, there's something new around each corner.

FEAR OF THE UNKNOWN

Acknowledging the limitations of our knowledge may open up possibilities of unpleasant surprises in our future. It's a can of worms that most people avoid. Fear of the unknown can, and has, stopped many creative people from sailing beyond their shore of knowledge. However, there is a distinction between imagined fear and real danger.

In a scene from the movie *After Earth*, actor Will Smith beautifully separated imagined fear and real danger when he said, "Fear is not real. The only place that fear can exist is in our thoughts of the future. It is a product of our imagination, causing us to fear things that do not and may not ever exist. Do not misunderstand me, danger is very real, but fear is a choice."

Our fear response to new information is a different type of threat than a lion chasing us. It doesn't threaten our lives. It threatens our beliefs, ideas, and perspectives. New information harnesses the power to shatter your reality. I understand. There's no need to rush. Take baby steps into new knowledge and experiences. The more you expand your mind, the less fear you'll feel. Committing to overcoming your fears is important because creative geniuses refuse to have limitations. Beyond your comfort zone is where curiosity and creativity will permeate every aspect of your life. Be open-minded to new and even radical possibilities. Expanding your worldview will give your mind more tools and, therefore, a greater ability to create something new and unique.

MY FAVORITE QUESTION

We tend to challenge our desires by asking, "Why?."

We're too inquisitive for our own good. Why should we do *this*? Why should we do *that*? It's a never-ending quest for answers.

Sometimes, asking "why" can become a trap. We get so caught up in searching for reasons and explanations that we lose sight of the possibilities that lie outside of those reasons. We become paralyzed, stuck in a cycle of overthinking and second-guessing.

Here's a simple, life-altering solution: Do not ask "Why?". Ask "Why not?".

Asking "why not" is a radical shift in perspective. It's a rebellious act against the limitations imposed by our constant need for explanations. "Why not" is the gateway to creativity, innovation, and personal growth. It opens up a world of possibilities that we may have never considered before. It challenges the status quo, defying conventional wisdom, and embracing the unknown. It breaks us free from limiting beliefs. We become the architects of our own lives, rather than passive observers.

Why do I stick to the traditional path? *Why not* explore alternative options and create my own unique path?

Why do I conform to societal expectations? *Why not* challenge societal norms and define my own version of success and happiness?

Why do I settle for a job I don't enjoy? *Why not* pursue a career that aligns with my passions and brings fulfillment?

Why do I have to stay in a toxic relationship? *Why not* prioritize my well-being and seek healthier, more fulfilling connections?

Why do I have to fear failure? *Why not* embrace failure as an opportunity for growth and learning?

Why don't I pursue my dreams? *Why not* take a leap of faith and actively pursue what brings me joy and fulfillment?

Why don't I step out of my comfort zone? *Why not* challenge myself and embrace new experiences that lead to personal growth?

Now, let me be clear: asking "why not" doesn't mean abandoning all sense of reason and logic. It is not about recklessness or impulsiveness. It's about questioning the assumptions and limitations that hold us back. It's about challenging the narratives we tell ourselves and expanding our horizons.

So, the next time you find yourself stuck in the endless loop of "Why?", take a step back and ask yourself, "Why not?." Embrace the uncertainties and the possibilities that lie beyond the confines of reason. *Why not* dare to explore the untapped potential within you?

COMPRESSING EXPERIENCES INTO CREATIONS

Author David Parell gave the perfect analogy of how experiences relate to creativity. He said that experiences become shareable creations like tree sap becomes maple syrup. It takes 50 gallons of sap to make one gallon of syrup.[7] So whenever you feel like you don't have enough

---

[7]   Parell, David. n.d. "Expression Is Compression." David Perell. https://perell.com/es say/expression-is-compression/.

ideas or inspiration to create something you're proud of, go collect more experiences. Fill up your gallons of sap. You may not know how everything will assemble, but it will.

Steve Jobs built on this concept, saying, "The key thing is that if you're going to make connections which are innovative, to connect two experiences together, then you have to not have the same bag of experiences as everyone else does or else you're going to make the same connections and then you won't be innovative. What you need to do is get different experiences than the normal course of events."

You can't unleash your creative potential with the same experiences as an everyday person. Change your usual routines. Pick up a new hobby. Attend classes and seminars on topics that you are unfamiliar with. Read books about opposing views. Travel the world. Creativity dies in the comfort zone, and travel is one of the best antidotes to comfort. Go places where they don't speak your language. Learn to communicate in new ways. This way of life is a prerequisite for all creative geniuses. Stop holding yourself back from accomplishing the things you want to do. Life is too short to be chained to what you know.

Key of Challenges

"The point is that there are challenges within techniques. When you differentiate in technique, you challenge yourself; you ask yourself the same question in a new way."— William Hurt

ENIGMATOLOGY

Enigmatology is the study and science of puzzles. It spans various genres: math, situational, word, mechanical, spot-the-difference, and more. Even though humans have been solving puzzles for at least as long as recorded history, the only person with a degree in enigmatology is Will Shortz. Shortz put his degree to good use. Shortz published over one hundred puzzle books and has been the puzzle editor at the New York Times since 1993. By April 2021, Shortz had edited over 10,000 crossword puzzles.

What fascinates me about enigmatology is the way each puzzle tests our creativity in unique ways. It amuses me that life feels like a massive enigmatology puzzle, where Shortz has crafted a series of highly personalized, immersive challenges for each of us to solve. There are real-world puzzles we face every day. It can be creating a fresh melody for your next song or theme of your next painting, but it can also be deciding what you want to do for your spouse's birthday or what you want to cook tonight for dinner. It's even in the struggle of finding a new job or starting a new business. Luckily there's a way to tactfully approach these creative challenges. Let's explore how.

BRAINSTORMING

BBDO is the world's most awarded advertising agency. Since 1891, BBDO built and pushed the stories behind infamous brands such as FedEx, AT&T, Visa, HP, GE, and many more. Alex Osborn was one of the five founders of BBDO and published several books on creative thinking. In his book *How To Think Up*, he presented the most popular creative problem-solving technique known today—brainstorming. BBDO's most successful advertising campaigns utilized his new innovative theory.

Alex partnered with Sid Parnes to develop the Osborn-Parnes Creative Problem Solving Process, the first formalized process for brainstorming ideas from problem to solution. This process can guide your creative thinking. It can help you find innovative solutions to improve your products, creations, craft, or relationships.

THREE CORE PRINCIPLES

Creative Problem Solving has three core principles you must stick to throughout the process.

First, you have to separate divergent and convergent thinking. Divergent thinking is when you create ideas without judgment. Convergent thinking is when you evaluate ideas. The problem is that most people try to do this simultaneously. Instead of thinking of one idea at a time and analyzing each to see if it will work, think of all fifty ideas first and then go back and analyze them. Convergent thinking interrupts the flow of ideas. Do both of them deeply, but separately.

Secondly, rephrase your challenges as open-ended questions. How can I make this painting proportional on a six-foot canvas? Why aren't my customers reordering my product? How can I make a cake that looks like a sneaker? Restructuring your problems utilizes your brain's natural trigger to solve challenges. Vaguely communicated problems tend to generate limited responses. If you dig deeper to ask the right question, your imagination will conjure up limitless ideas.

Thirdly, create a judgment-free zone. Judgment is a poison that will eat your problem solving journey from the inside out. When you attack ideas, your mind will start to build a wall of insecurity. This wall will block out novel ideas and solutions. Judgment kills great ideas before they ever see the light of day.

CREATIVE PROBLEM-SOLVING PROCESS

The framework for Creative Problem Solving is a four-step process. Start with clarifying and researching the problem. Gather as much information about your problem as possible. This information will be the tools you use in the next step. After you completely understand the problem, pose the problem as specific questions. Take the questions and research and use them as tools to generate ideas. Feel free to stray from your research, but don't completely ignore it. List every idea that's thrown out. Remember, this is a judgment-free zone. The next step is where you put back on your judgment hat. Define strict criteria for what makes an idea suitable. Evaluate and combine your ideas to pose solutions. Lastly, formulate and implement an action plan for the top prioritized solutions.

Great creative ideas are usually the outcome of tackling a specific problem. Brilliant minds don't wait for inspiration to come to them. Instead, they use laser-focused brainstorming. They concentrate on attempting to solve clearly defined problems. Understanding a problem, developing ideas to fix it, and assessing the most effective solutions is a key process to master. It's the backbone of creative problem-solving. This is at the core of all the strategies in this book. Creative geniuses have an uncontrollable urge to solve problems. You must nurture that quality in yourself, too. It will become second nature the more you exercise it.

* * *

Did any of these keys spark an interesting thought?
Share it with me at WorldOfCreatives.com

Key of Association

"So say whatever goes through your mind. Act as though, for instance, you were a traveler sitting next to the window of a railway carriage and describing to someone inside the carriage the changing views you see outside."—Sigmund Freud

GENERATING MILLION-DOLLAR CONTENT IDEAS

As of 2024, the wealthiest YouTuber is Jimmy Donaldson, commonly known as Mr. Beast. Every single one of his videos go viral, raking millions of views. He mastered content creation, and in an interview he shared his secret behind generating great ideas. He revealed that he uses a dictionary to pick random words to spark a new video concept. "It works actually better than you would think,"[8] he said. He explained that he does not limit himself to a dictionary. It's more about taking in random inspiration. Then he writes down what pops in his head, and "usually one out of every hundred is good." Odd connections breed genius ideas.

---

[8] YouTube - Marques Brownlee. (2021). 20 Questions with MrBeast! Retrieved January 9, 2024, from https://www.youtube.com/watch?v=SOq05_6w0ig.

FREE ASSOCIATION

Mr. Beast was using a technique called free association. Sigmund Freud, one of the greatest psychoanalysts of the modern era, coined the term free association. It was a form of therapy he used on his patients to help them gain uncanny realizations about themselves and their trauma. Freud had them say or express every thought, regardless of how irrelevant, silly, or painful it seemed. He let their thoughts and feelings flow without judgment. This method helped his patients find patterns in their thinking that were invisible to them. Freud didn't only use this technique to cure people with severe physical symptoms. He also helped others who felt "stuck" in any area of their lives.

Freud used free association as the therapeutic method of researching our unconscious mind, the storehouse of infinite ideas. Free association helps us produce new ideas through random word associations. It's about "ideas suggesting ideas." So one idea will trigger another idea, which will inspire another idea. Then it will continue to cycle until the process is over. Eventually, businesses adopted this strategy as a creative problem-solving technique. You can also use it to develop ideas in any creative field.

THE PRINCIPLE OF UNIVERSAL CONNECTION

Alexander Spirkin, a philosopher and psychologist who explored consciousness and the world around us, developed a mind-bending philosophy called the Principle of Universal Connection.

In his book *Dialectical Materialism*, he explained his concept of universal connection. He said, "Nothing in the world stands by itself. Every object is a link in an endless chain and is thus connected with all the other links. And this chain of the universe has never been broken; it unites all objects and processes in a single whole and thus has a universal character. We cannot move so much as our little finger without "disturbing" the whole universe. The life of the universe, its history lies in an infinite web of connections."[9]

This poetic philosophy observes that "everything is connected to everything else." This is why free association works so well. The Principle of Universal Connection is why we can make valuable connections between seemingly random objects. Exploring the link between two odd associations is an opportunity to find fresh ideas.

FLAT VS STEEP ASSOCIATIVE HIERARCHIES

Sarnoff Mednick is a psychologist that made major contributions to the field of creativity. He developed a theoretical model of the relationship between free association and creativity. Mednick defined the process of creative thinking as "the forming of associative elements into new combinations which either meet specific requirements or are in some way useful. The more mutually remote the elements of the new combination, the more creative the process or solution." He developed a model of grading creativity based on this definition. Imagine the infinite range of ideas that can come from associating two objects. The more obvious the connection, the less creative the idea is. The more novel the connection, the more creative it is. Mednick ranked these ideas based on what he called associative hierarchies. He argued that creative people have flat associative hierarchies meaning they can easily access distant, remote associations. Less creative people have a steep associative hierarchy. Closer, more common associative ideas cross their minds. For example, if given the word "watch", he

---

[9] Spirkin, Alexander. 1983. "The Principle of Universal Connection and Development." Www.marxists.org. Progress Publishers. 1983. https://www.marxists.org/reference/archive/spirkin/works/dialectical-materialism/ch02-s05.html.

argued that less creative people would say typical associations like "time." In contrast, creative people would be more likely to say remote associations such as "out" or "band."

A great example of this is the popular TV show Family Feud. In each episode, Steve Harvey quizzes an everyday family. Each question starts with the phrase, "We surveyed one hundred people. The top ten answers are on the board." This game is challenging because they order the top ten answers from most common to least common. The top three answers are usually the easiest. After that, your mind must reach further into the abyss to make more novel connections.

Mednick developed a creativity test based on his theory called the Remote Associates Test (RAT). The RAT test shows you a long list of three seemingly unrelated words. The goal is to think of one word that ties the other three words together in a limited amount of time. Here are three examples:

Fish. Mine. Rush. = ______.

Call. Pay. Line. = ______.

Motion. Poke. Down. = ______.

The answers are in the footnotes.[10]

Practice free association to flatten your associative hierarchy. When someone is known for always having good ideas, it's because they can quickly access ideas that exist beyond the realm of usual thought patterns.

Let's put it into practice. Identify a problem. It could be a problem within your business or a new idea for a painting series. Anything. Grab a dictionary and list out random words. Mix in words that are both related and unrelated to your problem. As you read the list, your brain will scan for useful analogies between the random word and your problem. Let your thoughts flow. Don't dwell on whether your

---

[10] The answers are: Gold, Phone, and Slow.

conclusions make sense. Hidden within each analogy is a creative idea or potential solution. Follow this method to spark novel ideas.

Key of Systems

"Just as we develop our physical muscles through overcoming opposition, such as lifting weights, we develop our character muscles by overcoming challenges and adversity."—Stephen Covey

ELON MUSK

Creative challenges are complicated to solve. This makes the need for a sound plan to attack these challenges even more pressing. This is where the idea of mental systems step in.

Mental systems serve as scaffolding for your thoughts. They help you break down complex challenges into simpler ones, allowing your mind to work through them rather than drowning in anxiety. Think of them as ways to protect yourself from mental noise to make the best decisions possible with limited knowledge. This concept helped Elon Musk. Elon went from being a self-taught scientist to founding arguably the most important and profitable companies of our era— PayPal, Tesla, SpaceX, and Neuralink.

In 2002, Elon Musk had the ambitious idea to send humanity's first manned-rocket to Mars. The first thing he needed for this mission was a rocket suitable for spaceflight. He approached several rocket manufacturing companies and, to his dismay, found that it was expensive to build them. The average cost was over $60 million. This was when he took this problem and applied his go-to mental system, first principle thinking.

In an interview, he revealed how he applied this mental system to get around the high prices of purchasing a pre-made space rocket. He said, "I tend to approach things from a physics framework. Physics teaches you to reason from first principles rather than by analogy. So, I said, okay, let's look at the first principles. What is a rocket made of? Aerospace-grade aluminum alloys, plus some titanium, copper, and carbon fiber. Then I asked, what is the value of those materials on the commodity market? It turned out that the materials cost of a rocket was around 2% of the typical price." The other 98% of the costs came from the inability to reuse the rocket after it's launched. The multi-million dollar rocket is left floating in space.

In another interview, he compared it to commercial airlines. "If aircraft were not reusable and you needed a new one for every flight, then each ticket would cost millions of dollars, at least. One way. And you'd need two for a two-way trip. And almost no one would be able to afford to fly."

This led to a clear answer to the creative challenge. Rather than purchasing pre-made rockets at astronomical rates, Elon decided to form a company, SpaceX. They acquired the materials he needed at affordable prices and started building reusable rockets. SpaceX eventually successfully designed them, bringing space launches down to a tiny fraction of the industry's typical costs. As a result of Elon's first principles thinking, we can witness commercial space travel today.

FIRST PRINCIPLE THINKING

The Greek philosopher Aristotle described first principles as "the first basis from which a thing is known." First principle thinking is a way to take a step back and look at things from a fresh perspective. It's approaching creative problems by breaking them down into their most basic and fundamental parts. Then, you can evaluate the pieces to find alternative solutions or ways to reach your goal.

As the famous military strategist John Boyd explained, think about any three objects, such as a sailboat, a tank, and a tricycle. Break them down into parts, and then see if you can combine components from each to create something new. You can make a snowmobile, for instance, if you combine parts in one particular order. Another arrangement may give you an armored boat, and so on. This is how first principles thinking works—first deconstruct, then reconstruct. Once you have a solid foundation of baseline knowledge, you can improve each element before reassembling it.

SIX THINKING HATS SYSTEM

Another mental system that builds on these ideas is Edward de Bono's Six Thinking Hats system. This mental system teaches you how to juggle different kinds of thinking to achieve creative clarity. Each different type of thinking is paired with one out of six imaginary hats. The objective is to wear only one hat at a time while embodying the creative character of that hat. Cycling through all the hats helps you look at your problem from every angle. This mental system works beautifully with groups of people. Assign each person a hat that matches their natural strengths and watch the magic work. Let's look at these hats in greater detail:

White Hat is factual thinking. It involves focusing completely on the facts of the problem, using data that is available.

Red Hat is emotional thinking. Examine your gut feelings and see what messages they are sending up to you. Powerful intuition is your tool.

Black Hat is pessimism. Playing the Devil's advocate allows you to attempt to reveal flaws that need improvement. This will make your solutions to your creative challenges more multifaceted and cautious.

Yellow Hat is positive thinking. This helps provide the hope and motivation needed to carry tasks to completion. Identifying the best-case scenarios will help you respond to unexpected success with speed and efficiency.

Green Hat requires divergent thinking. Scale back self-imposed rules and constraints to work with the flaws identified by the Black Hat. Examine the challenge from different perspectives, and find novel combinations of ideas from other domains.

Blue Hat is responsible for shifting between all the hats and 'running the show,' so to speak. After you gave all the hats their moment to shine, combine everything you learned into one concrete solution.

SCAMPER

SCAMPER is another effective creative mental model. It's a question-based process pioneered by Bob Eberle and used to solve problems and ignite creativity during company brainstorming meetings.

SCAMPER stands for:

- Substitute
- Combine
- Adapt
- Modify
- Put to another use

- Eliminate
- Reverse

These keywords represent the questions you ask yourself along your creative journey. You do not have to follow these questions in order. SCAMPER is considered one of the most straightforward idea generation models to follow. That's because it's based on one simple idea: Every new idea is a modification of existing old ideas. With this technique, you can generate ideas without drifting far from the original topic. Below are the seven SCAMPER questions. Once you identify your goal, fill in the blank with your idea, product, business, project, or creative challenge:

- **Substitute:** What can I substitute or change about _________ to achieve my desired goal? What resources, processes, rules, or use-cases can I change about _________?
- **Combine:** How can I combine two or more parts of _________ to achieve a different _________? Can I combine concepts, goals, and resources?
- **Adapt:** What can I adapt in _________ to achieve my desired goal? What can I adapt, readjust, emulate, or pull inspiration from?
- **Modify:** What can I modify about _________ to achieve my desired goal? How could you change the shape, look, or feel? What could you emphasize or highlight?
- **Put to Another Use:** What are new ways to use _________ to achieve my desired goal?
- **Eliminate:** What can I eliminate or simplify in _________ to achieve my desired goal? What can I streamline, eliminate, tone down, or make smaller, faster, lighter, or more fun?
- **Reverse:** How can I change, reorder, or reverse the _________ to achieve my desired goal? What changes would be made if you

tried to do the exact opposite of what you're trying to do now?

PROCESS-BASED THINKING

If you want to change the way you create, change your thinking. There are infinite ways to adjust your thinking. These are a few that have been stress tested by other creative geniuses. These cheat codes instantly improve your thinking. So, the next time you or your team face any creative block, try to work with these mental tools. Dig until you obtain core truths, challenge them, and work your way up.

Key of Documentation

RICHARD BRANSON

While Sir Richard Branson struggled with dyslexia in 1950, few, besides his adoring mother, could have imagined the heights he would achieve in the entrepreneurial world. He is arguably the World's Most Interesting Man. His reported net worth is around the $4 billion mark from building an empire called Virgin Group. Virgin Group spans many industries and includes over 200 businesses. He also left his mark on the world by tackling a handful of bold feats. In 1987, he broke a world record by crossing the Atlantic in a hot-air balloon. A year later, he drove a military tank through Times Square. Throughout all his success, Sir Richard played a vital part in global philanthropy with Nelson Mandela. He's also the author of six books and finds time to surf, kite, and play tennis with his family.

A key to his success is revealed in the advice he gives the most: carry a notebook. In a 2006 interview, Sir Richard said, "It may sound ridiculous, but my most important advice is to always carry a little notebook in your back pocket. I think the number one thing that I take with me when I'm traveling is the notebook...I could never have built the Virgin Group into the size it is without those few bits of paper."[11]

Sir Richard advocates his predisposition for list-making in his books and blog. He uses these lists to "give shape" and form to his visions. He goes through a pile of notebooks a year, writing lists ranging from small goals to outlandish challenges. Sir Richard credits the meteoric success of many Virgin Group companies to a random spark that originated in one of these notebooks. "Write down every single idea you have, no matter how big or small," he says, "You never know what's going to hit."

HANDWRITTEN NOTES

Sir Richard isn't the only successful creative with a strong habit of daily note-taking. Creative giants such as Mark Twain, George Lucas, Ludwig van Beethoven, and Thomas Edison shared a robust love for carrying little notebooks everywhere they went. Leonardo da Vinci's notes were so sacred to him that he wrote them using special codes. He also wrote in reverse, mirroring his handwriting, to make it difficult for others to read. He only wrote in the traditional direction when the text was intended for others to read. In 1994, Bill Gates paid $30.8 million for Leonardo da Vinci's notebook at an auction. It was the most expensive book ever sold.

A more modern example comes from researching Drake, one of the most successful and influential artists in hip-hop and pop music. Like da Vinci, he keeps a private notepad that is the starting ground of his hit songs. "I keep a constant notepad of just ideas, play by play," he said in an interview. "If you read through that notepad you could really see where my mind is at. Where my life is at. But nobody is allowed

---

[11] Kruse, K. (2017, March 15). Richard Branson's single most important tool. LEADx. https://leadx.org/articles/richard-bransons-single-important-tool/

to read that notepad." What benefits about writing in a notebook do creative geniuses know that most people don't?

Turns out, science supports handwritten note-taking, too. You may be tempted to take digital notes in today's tech-driven world. Digital notes are great to store your thoughts and ideas in a searchable way. I'm also an advocate for digital notes, but while taking notes on my phone makes storage, safety, and self-expression convenient, it isn't as cognitively beneficial as writing notes by hand. Research by Pam Mueller of Princeton University suggests that "when people type their notes, they have this tendency to try to take verbatim notes and write down as much of the lecture as they can. The students who were taking longhand notes in our studies were forced to be more selective—because you can't write as fast as you can type. And that extra processing of the material that they were doing benefited them."[12] Although the study was in a classroom context, the research holds true in other walks of life. Writing out things by hand forces you to process your thoughts in real-time. This engages your mind much better than any digital medium could. When generating ideas, use pen and paper. When storing and building on your ideas, use technology.

THE EBBINGHAUS CURVE

In 1885, Hermann Ebbinghaus developed The Ebbinghaus Curve, commonly known as the Curve of Forgetting. His study tracked how memory diminishes over time. His findings illustrated a chart of the speed memories slip from our brains if we don't revisit the information. You might've experienced the Curve of Forgetting when you were

---

12 Mueller, Pam A., and Daniel M. Oppenheimer. 2014. "The Pen Is Mightier than the Keyboard: Advantages of Longhand over Laptop Note Taking." Psychological Science 25 (6): 1159–68. https://doi.org/10.1177/0956797614524581.

learning a new skill. Maybe you spent a month or two learning a new language, but a few days slacking off set you back weeks.

Based on his findings, our immediate memory recall is nearly 100%. However, if we don't revisit our notes, we will forget about 40% over the first 24 hours. If we wait another 24 hours, we'll lose 60%. Thirty days later, we will forget 90%.[13]

It pains me to think about all the ideas I've had in my life that vanished because I never wrote them down. Unfortunately, our brains operate on a strict use it or lose it policy. If you want to increase your idea retention, you have to revisit your notes.

TIME-TRAVELING

I usually process how I think by writing notes. I've written 5070 notes dating back a decade, and counting. That means, on average, I wrote more than once daily for the last ten years. And I'm not talking about to-do lists and reminders. My notes are scattered with fleshed-out business ideas, studies I've researched, poems about life, love letters, memos to my future kids, shower thoughts, movie scripts, book notes, art show concepts, and random mind-blowing information I learned, to name a few. Writing has become one of my go-to ways to process my thoughts.

Notes give you the ability to time travel by unlocking detailed memories, thoughts, and emotions. Writing coach David Parell teaches this concept by referencing the habits of songwriter and poetic genius Kendrick Lamar.[14] Kendrick Lamar once explained how note-

---

[13] Roth, Jim. 2020. "THE CURVE of FORGETTING." Spokane.edu. 2020. http://ol.sc c.spokane.edu/jroth/Courses/English%2094-study%20skills/MASTER%20DOCS% 20and%20TESTS/Curve%20of%20Forgetting.htm.

[14] Parell, David. n.d. "Note-Taking Is Time Travel." David Perell. Accessed June 7, 2023. https://perell.com/note/note-taking-is-time-travel/.

taking is the closest thing we have to time travel:

> *"I have to make notes because a lot of my inspiration comes from meeting people or going outside the country, or going around the corner of my old neighborhood and talking to a five-year-old little boy. And I have to remember these things. I have to write them down and then five or three months later, I have to find that same emotion that I felt when I was inspired by it, so I have to dig deep to see what triggered the idea... It comes back because I have key little words that make me realize the exact emotion which drew the inspiration."*

Kendrick Lamar's goal with note-taking is to capture the essence of moments that impact him. When it's time for him to write a song, he has an endless source of inspiration. His notebook has everything he needs. He uses them to mentally and emotionally time travel to relive his experiences. When you listen to his music, you transport through time with him. This is the effect of powerful note-taking habits integrated into your creative passion.

CULTIVATING NOTE-TAKING

To get the most out of note-taking, start by developing a system. Think of note-taking as a secret language between your conscious and unconscious mind. Any system works as long as it is consistent and unique to you. Feel free to use a lingo only you understand, reflecting your unique way of processing information.

When an idea strikes, jot everything down. Don't leave anything for later. Despite our best intentions, we forget things faster than we'd like to admit. So, don't leave remembering inspiration up to chance.

Don't neglect your ideas. Set aside time to review your thoughts and elaborate on them. This will drastically increase your idea retention and separate you from other creators.

Lastly, use your notes for inspiration. Creative people feel the burden of unexpressed musings, ideas, and emotions. Don't let your ideas go to waste. Use your notes to fuel your inspiration when you're running on E.

Key of Continuing

"Innovation is saying no to a thousand things."—Steve Jobs

YOUR FIRST IDEA

In a 1961 experiment, researchers tasked participants with generating a list of ideas to solve a creative problem in five minutes. Then the researchers filtered the ideas through a rating and evaluation criteria. The results showed that the ideas listed during the second half, were significantly better than those from the first. Also, there was a correlation between the top ranking ideas coming from the participants who gave the most responses.[15]

The phenomenon suggests that the mind first explores the most obvious solutions before delving into more innovative or less conventional ideas. This is the danger of gravitating toward the first idea that pops up in your head. It denies you the opportunity to find more creative solutions. Innovation does not occur at the beginning of the creative process. It's the end result. Move beyond the first batch of ideas so more novel ideas can materialize. Your best ideas are often your last ideas.

---

[15] Parnes, S. J. (1961). Effects of extended effort in creative problem solving. Journal of Educational Psychology, 52(3), 117–122. https://doi.org/10.1037/h0044650

When you think you've reached the end of your creative thinking process, push through and think some more. Most creators underestimate the value of persistence in their creative journey. Creative geniuses know that their best ideas painfully lie on the other side of what's obvious. This is the true definition of thinking outside the box.

CREATIVE CLIFF ILLUSION

Brian Lucas, a professor of organizational behavior, conducted eight studies on people's creative process. He started the experiments by asking the participants to predict how their levels of creativity change over time. They predicted their creativity would decline, but the results revealed their output was more creative over time. Brian calls this the creative-cliff illusion, the misconception people have that creativity decreases over time, even though it tends to rise.[16]

Brian challenges the assumption that our best ideas stem from our freshest thinking. He advocates being patient with your creative thought process to give your mind time to let your best ideas emerge. Don't give in to the pressure of cutting your creative process short. Great ideas come to those who persevere.

EINSTELLUNG EFFECT

In chess, a smothered mate is a popular checkmate strategy. It's achieved by placing the knight where the checkmated king can't move because it's completely surrounded by its own pieces. Researchers Merim Bilali and Peter McLeod used this chess technique to conduct

---

[16] Lucas, Brian J., and Loran F. Nordgren. 2020. "The Creative Cliff Illusion." Proceedings of the National Academy of Sciences 117 (33): 19830–36. https://doi.o rg/10.1073/pnas.2005620117.

one of the most insightful studies on cognitive bias. They gave master chess players a board that had two potential solutions. They could either win by checkmating their opponent in five steps with the well-known smothered mate or, instead, they could win with a faster three-step solution. They challenged each player to checkmate their opponent as quickly as possible. Once the master players noticed the smothered mate was possible, they were incapable of noticing the quicker three-step strategy. They ignored a more efficient solution in favor of a more familiar solution. Then something shocking happened. They showed them a nearly identical board with one piece moved, making the smothered mate no longer an option. The players immediately recognized the faster solution.[17]

This is the Einstellung effect, a psychological phenomenon where our preexisting knowledge stops us from seeing to the best solutions. This effect leaves us cognitively incapable of separating our previous experiences from the current problem we're facing. In an attempt to be more efficient, our brain refers to past solutions instead of giving the current situation enough thought.

THE LAW OF THE INSTRUMENT

In 1966 psychologist Abraham Maslow said, "I suppose it is tempting, if the only tool you have is a hammer, to treat everything as if it were a nail." The law of the instrument[18], otherwise known as Maslow's hammer, refers to a major consequence of the Einstellung effect. People want to use the same tool for every problem.

---

[17] Arra, Stephen. 2021. "Einstellung Effect: What You Already Know Can Hurt You." Www.exaptive.com. May 17, 2021. https://www.exaptive.com/blog/einstellung-eff ect-0.

[18] "Law of the Instrument." n.d. The Decision Lab. https://thedecisionlab.com/biases/ law-of-the-instrument.

One of the most harmful examples of the law of the instrument is the education system. It's built as a one-size-fits-all hammer when there's a wide variety of ways kids and teens learn. Instead, there should be an array of approaches to cater to their unique needs.

Someone with only a hammer will try to fix everything without seeking better alternatives. Over time, fixing things with a hammer becomes the norm, and norms are hard to escape. Don't try to squeeze problems within the bounds of your skillset. Identify the skills required to execute the best solution.

Every problem is unique. Be open to using a different tool, method, or way of thinking to solve it. Knowing when our skills are applicable is useful because the law of the instrument can cause tunnel vision. Don't always fall victim to your instincts. Your first draft, idea, or plan of action is probably not the best you can do. If you believe it is, put it to the test by painfully persisting along your creative journey beyond your predisposed limitations. That's where creative geniuses find gold.

Key of Stealing

"Good artists copy, great artists steal."—Pablo Picasso

WHO FOUNDED CUBISM?

The famous Spanish painter Pablo Picasso created artwork that stands in a league of its own. He grew up painting realistic portraits of people because it was the style of the time. Eventually, he grew dissatisfied with realism and began experimenting with new techniques.

In his 20s, Picasso was introduced to different cultures' artwork. While European traditionalists dubbed different cultures' art as primitive and unworthy of creative critique, Picasso rejected this way of thinking. He grew so enamored with African art, especially storytelling masks, that he took on their unique painting style. This style didn't represent reality as it was. His art transformed reality into sharp, shocking, alien objects. He deformed and fragmented the human figure. His choice of color and brushstrokes created a new visual vocabulary within a few years. This style, later known as Cubism, inspired a radical change in modern art that continues to this day. When asked about the nature of his work, he said, "The world today doesn't make sense, so why should I paint pictures that do?".

Even though I admire Picasso's work and his quote, "Good artists copy, great artists steal," I hesitated about including Picasso as an example in this chapter. The more I researched the history of Cubism, the more I questioned his ethics.

In 1920, when asked about African influence, Pablo Picasso said, "African art? Never heard of it!". Yet, documentation shows that Henri Matisse exposed Picasso to an African and Oceanic art collection. Picasso later spoke about the experience saying, "And then I understood what painting really meant. It's not an aesthetic process; it's a form of magic that interposes itself between us and the hostile universe…That day I understood that I had found my path."[19]

Some people argue that Picasso wouldn't have been a renowned creative genius if he didn't steal from anonymous African artists. Suppose Picasso did mimic the art styles of African artwork and denied it. In that case, it could be considered cultural appropriation instead of truly stealing like an artist. Pulling inspiration while belittling those who inspired you is disrespectful. Inspiration is a gift worth appreciating. Let's explore the concept of ethically stealing like an artist.

A CAREER BUILT ON IMPERSONATION

Although comedy is highly subjective, everybody can agree on one thing. The laughter that ensues when a comedian nails an impression of another person is unmatched. Impressions combine every element of a comedian's creative muscle. The impression may have an observational angle, examining and acting out someone's exact characteristics. It could be more caricature, wildly exaggerating everything about the person. It forces them to pay close attention to every aspect of

---

[19] Gwaambuka, Tatenda. 2019. "European Great, Pablo Picasso Stole the Work of African Artists but Would Not Acknowledge Them." The African Exponent. January 3, 2019. https://www.africanexponent.com/post/9608-pablo-picasso-stole-the-wo rk-of-african-artists.

another person—how they walk, talk, use their hands, dress, smile, and laugh. These data points are then synthesized brilliantly into a recognizable impression. This blend of 'originality' and 'stealing' gives impersonations its comedic power.

One of the famous masters of this craft is Kenan Thompson, the longest-running cast member of *Saturday Night Live (SNL)*, the world's most famous sketch comedy show of all time. Kenan first honed his mimicry skills on Nickelodeon shows such as *All That* and *Kenan and Kel*. At age 25, Kenan auditioned and was accepted as an SNL cast member. As of 2024, he has since shot 21 seasons of the show. His rebelliousness, silliness, and precise, spot-on mimicry, mark his artistic style. Throughout his career, he has masterfully performed impressions of social icons such as Al Sharpton, Gary Coleman, Serena Williams, and Chaka Khan.

THE BOOK'S TITLE

I should probably address the elephant in the room: *48 Keys of Creativity* sounds a lot like *48 Laws of Power* by Robert Greene. Well, Robert did not write this book. It's not affiliated with him at all.

The truth is I did not choose this title out of spitefulness. I did it out of admiration. I'm a fan of Robert Greene. If you want to learn a topic, learn it from someone obsessed with it. When I read *48 Laws of Power*, I gravitated towards Robert's obsession over understanding power dynamics and finding the connections between historical figures and human nature, then using thought-provoking analysis to create actionable advice anyone can apply to become more powerful.

His passion for power reminded me of my love for creativity, so I used that inspiration as a guide. I studied the lives of over one hundred creative geniuses, read countless books and research studies, and made deep comparisons. I documented my learnings into 48 comprehensive keys, just as I imagined Robert would've advised.

For that reason, this book wouldn't exist if it wasn't for Robert Greene. In fact, he was one of the many authors I drew inspiration from to write this book. I combined Robert Greene's framework, Malcolm Gladwell's method of connecting seemingly unrelated dots, James Clear's book cover layout and simplistic writing style, Mark Manson's bold book titles and blunt self-help advice, and Ryan Holiday's philosophical breakthroughs, to name a few. These creators inspired *Create or Die: 48 Keys of Creativity*. Without them, I wouldn't have mustered up the courage to write a word. They mentored me even though I never met them. Each of them deserve their flowers.

Through the lens of these greats, I discovered my writing style. Stealing, when done respectfully, is one of the many ways creative geniuses execute their visions at the highest level.

STEALING LIKE AN ARTIST

So, what makes Kenan Thompson such a master impressionist? When describing his famous impression of Steve Harvey, Kenan told Steve, "I feel the 'real' in you, and I've just been around you so much. I watch how you walk, and I watch how you deliver stuff; the passion that you have, especially when you're delivering jokes. You throw that energy on something that you're trying to get across in a certain kind of way. Especially on stage…I just watch you do you to the utmost, and then I try to give it back."

That quote expresses a key idea in creativity: Artists function as mirrors more than light sources. Some of the best art arises when artists steal from one another rather than striving for originality. Stealing, however, doesn't mean plagiarizing. The latter is the shameless and unethical copying of someone's hard-earned idea and plastering your name on it. That kind of stealing is not what makes a creative genius.

The kind of stealing we are talking about is the mirroring Kenan hinted at. It involves taking the essence of something creative, reworking or remixing it, and allowing it to shine a light on our unique artistic voice. As the legendary poet, T. S. Eliot said, "Immature poets imitate; mature poets steal; bad poets deface what they take, and good poets make it into something better, or at least something different." Creative stealing is not just borrowing an idea. It's a process of evolution that uses the idea or combines multiple ideas in new, unexpected ways. It happens all around us, even if we don't see it. Drake is one of the top music artists and a lot of his beats build on top of old songs. If you listen to Timmy Thomas' song *Why Can't We Live Together*, you can hear how it influenced Drake's song *Hotline Bling*. The famous rock band Led Zeppelin immortalized many old blues songs by reinventing them. Even the great Albert Einstein worked at a patent office, looking to patents to develop his ideas. That's where he built upon the works of physicists and mathematicians such as Hendrik Lorentz and Henri Poincaré. Kobe Bryant mimicked the movements of Michael Jordan, the greatest basketball player of all-time, until he developed his own play style. Steve Jobs copied the innovation tactics of Edwin Land, the brilliant mind behind Polaroid. Beyonce's iconic *Single Ladies* music video choreography was based on a Bob Fosse routine in a video from 1969. Great thinkers know how to recognize, copy, and evolve the tactics of other great thinkers.

Here's how you can ethically put this law into motion. First, find someone whose craft you admire. Then, imitate. Copy over their drawings, line by line, stroke by stroke. Play their compositions note for note. Spend hours in front of the mirror to ensure your body traces the exact movements they do as you dance. Write with the same rhyme scheme they use. A famous technique called "copywork" teaches people how to write better by having them copy word for word, line by line, other authors' best work.

Once you've imitated long enough, you'll notice certain elements you want to adopt. You'll also start to stray from their framework. Listen to your intuition. It's your unique creative spirit speaking to you. That's when you'll know that you've arrived at something new and yours. Creative geniuses embody various elements of their idols combined into one creator. Our failure to become those we admire expose what makes us truly unique.

* * *

Did any of these keys spark an interesting thought?
Share it with me at WorldOfCreatives.com

Key of Visualization

"I believe that visualization is one of the most powerful means of achieving personal goals."—Harvey Mackay

JIM CARREY

Actor Jim Carrey is no stranger to the art of visualization. During an interview with Oprah, he spoke about how he visualized achieving his goals. Early in his career, he didn't have a lot of money. Jim was hungry for success. He went to the top of a hill on Mulholland Drive and pictured the things he wanted. He imagined directors interested in his work and his idols praising him. He told himself he already had these things. At the time, he wasn't conscious of how powerful this technique was, but he did it daily to keep his spirits high.

In an interview with Oprah, Jim Carrey told the story of his most famous visualization. While struggling to find gigs and progress in his career, he made a bold decision: he wrote himself a check for ten million dollars. He made it out to "Jim Carrey. For acting services rendered." Then he dated it for Thanksgiving 1995, giving himself 3 years to achieve it. He folded the check and put it in his wallet as a constant reminder of his end goal. Jim acknowledged that dreams like this don't magically come true. Oprah explained that "visualization works if you work hard," and the actor agreed, saying, "Well, yeah.

That's the thing, you can't just visualize and then, you know, go eat a sandwich." It takes hard work and laser focus on a specific goal.

He worked harder on his craft and continued auditioning. On Thanksgiving 1995, Jim Carrey received confirmation that he would make ten million dollars for his role in the classic movie *Dumb and Dumber*.

THE POWER OF VISUALIZATION

When asked about visualization, Jim Carrey said, "Whenever I wanted something to happen, I manifested it. I stood there in an open field like this, with my arms out." This sounds too good to be true. Well, it is. Visualizing the end goal won't make you magically move mountains with your thoughts. If you can move things with your mind, stay put, the CIA will be knocking down your front door within the next minute. The power of visualization doesn't directly change the world. The power comes from the way it changes your mind.

In a well-known study about visualization, sports psychologist Judd Biasiotto split basketball students into three groups to improve their free-throw shooting.[20]

The first group didn't practice or think about free throws. They couldn't even touch a basketball. The second group of players went to the gym every day and practiced free throws for half an hour. The third group went to the gym every day and spent half an hour with their eyes closed, visualizing making every free throw. They imagined feeling the ball's texture in their hands' grip and shooting with proper form.

---

[20] Haefner, Joe. 2018. "Mental Rehearsal & Psychology Aspects of Basketball - Visualization." Breakthrough Basketball. 2018. https://www.breakthroughbas ketball.com/mental/visualization.html.

After 30 days, Judd tested the players. The results were astounding. The first group showed no improvement. The second group improved by 24%. The third group improved by 23%. That means that the group that only visualized shooting improved nearly the same as the group that physically practiced.

Visualization changes what you achieve by changing your mind. Oprah Winfrey said, "Anything you can imagine, you can create." Imagination does not create things, but it primes your body and mind to pursue anything. Visualization helps you believe in yourself. When you imagine yourself accomplishing grand creative feats, you see in your mind that it's possible.

VALUE TAGGING

Throughout life, we soak in tons of information. We meet people, visit places, experience things, and learn about various topics. Value tagging is the process our brain uses to assign importance to all the information we're exposed to.[21]

Value tags dictate how we navigate life at an unconscious level. We filter through our value tags before we take every action. There are logical tags that relate to our survival and emotional tags that relate to our aspirations. Survival value tags could be memories than warn you to stay away from fire or even a negative customer service experience with a brand. An emotional value tag could be the feeling you had winning an award or the taste of your favorite food.

Value tags can be damaging because it's easy to assign a high value to things we fear. For example, suppose a person goes through a painful

---

[21] Swart, Tara. 2001. "What Is Value Tagging? | Psychology Today." Www.psychologytoday.com. October 14, 2001. https://www.psychologytoday. com/us/blog/faith-in-science/201910/what-is-value-tagging.

breakup. They might add negative value tags to healthy traits about that person that can interfere when selecting future relationships.

The good news is that we can also assign a disproportionately high value to things we care about. If we can convince our subconscious to attach a high-value tag to our visualizations, it will influence our actions until we achieve our vision. Carl Jung said, "Until you make the unconscious conscious, it will direct your life, and you will call it fate."

VISION STACK

Well, how do we apply value tagging and visualization to our creative journey? It's done by creating a vision stack for your creative endeavors. A vision stack combines photos, videos, audio, and text, conveying the end goal. You can make a vision stack of runway show videos, fabric swatches, sketches from top designers, and mood boards to bring your high-end fashion collection to life. If you dream of creating a feature film, your vision stack could draw inspiration from various cinematic styles, iconic movie scenes, and award-winning set designs. You can pull sounds from different songs, lyrical themes, storytelling techniques, and album covers to create a vision stack for your next album. These vision stacks will give your mind exactly what it needs to prioritize the end goal. I designed the cover for this book before I started writing it. It made the book feel real to me years before I completed it.

Now that you made your vision stack, look at it every day. Add to it when you think about new ideas. Share it when people are struggling to understand your vision. Your mind increases your vision's value the more you look at your vision stack. Ralph Waldo Emerson said, "We become what we think about all day long." If you can think of it, you can create it.

Key of Process

"Beginnings are usually scary, and endings are usually sad, but it's everything in between that makes it all worth living."—Bob Marley

BRYAN CRANSTON

When I researched persistent creators, the famous American actor Bryan Cranston of *Malcolm in the Middle* and *Breaking Bad* stood out. In his memoir, *A Life in Parts*, he talked about his dissatisfaction with his creative life early in his career. He hustled from audition to audition, making a steady living but felt stuck. A lot of his feelings stemmed from a place of unfulfilled expectations. This is one of the main problems with an excessively goal-oriented approach to creativity. He would set his mind to a goal, such as getting an acting gig, scoring a temporary contract, or earning a specific amount of money. Then, whenever he didn't meet those goals, it would leave him with resentment that chipped at his motivation to pursue his creative dreams.

At a pivotal moment in his career, his mentor, Breck Costin, suggested that Bryan make a small change in how he approached his creative journey. He told Bryan to switch his attention from focusing on goals to focusing on the creative process. This seemingly minor shift in focus hugely impacted Bryan's creative life. He learned that when a creator lets go of their attachment to the results of their actions, they find joy in the action itself. The expectations and need for validation stemming from excessive goals disappeared. He found himself able to relax and be fully present wherever he was. Serenity and freedom replaced his endless urge to succeed. Bryan wrote, "Once I made the switch, I had power in any room I walked into. Which meant I could relax. I was free."

He learned a valuable lesson about creative genius: Focus on the process. After this switch, he managed to land a major role in the three-time Emmy-nominated series *Malcolm in the Middle*. He later starred in one of my favorite series, *Breaking Bad*, winning him four Emmys.

LOCUS OF CONTROL

Psychologist Julian Rotter explained this facet of human behavior with his theory called Locus of Control. Locus of Control (LOC) is the amount of control people feel they have over the events influencing their lives. He described it as a spectrum with one end representing an internal LOC and the other being external. People with a more internal LOC derive inspiration to act from within themselves. They perceive themselves as having the ability to create positive changes in their lives and associate their successes or failures with their own choices. On the other hand, people favoring a more external LOC often see themselves as powerless. They attribute the flow of their lives to forces beyond their control, whether it is luck, systems, or people more powerful than them. According to Rotter, when people with an internal LOC succeed, they attribute their success to their abilities. If they fail, they blame it on a lack of sufficient effort on their part. People with an external LOC tend to associate their successes with their tasks being easy while blaming their failures on bad luck.

As long as we position ourselves at the mercy of our goals, we latch to an external Locus of Control. Attributing our success to the accomplishment of a goal robs us of our creativity and imagination. It causes us to experiment less. It applies pressure to taking creative leaps. However, focusing on the process has the opposite effect. Once we enjoy the act of creation, we bring our more free-flowing side to every opportunity. We move with confidence and ease towards demands placed on our creativity. We have fun, experiment, and engage deeply with the experience. We embrace creativity without worrying about its results. This kind of internal freedom is rare. A process-focused mentality creates the ecosystem that allows us to succeed creatively long-term.

PROCESS x EFFORT = RESULTS

Progress inevitably happens when you stay focused on the process. In Lebron James' post-game interview after securing the 2020 NBA Championship with the LA Lakers, he said, "The most fulfilling thing, besides seeing my teammates as happy as they are, is being able to know that you can put in the work, literally trust the process, live by the process, and then see the results." The key to focusing on the journey is honing in on the right process for your craft.

I know I stressed the importance of visualization in another key of creativity, but I'm about to throw a curve-ball. There's a study from 1998 involving three groups of students studying for exams.[22] Every day, before studying, each group had a five-minute visualization session. Group 1 visualized the process they would use to study,

---

[22] Taylor, S. E., L. B. Pham, I. D. Rivkin, and D. A. Armor. 1998. "Harnessing the Imagination. Mental Simulation, Self-Regulation, and Coping." The American Psychologist 53 (4): 429–39. https://doi.org/10.1037//0003-066x.53.4.429.

including reviewing their notes, turning off the TV, and rejecting invitations to go out. Group 2 visualized themselves looking at the list of grades posted on the wall and seeing that they received an A on the exam. Group 3 didn't receive any instructions.

The results were intriguing. Group 1 started studying earlier, studied for longer hours, and scored 8 points higher on their exam than the other two groups. After multiple tests, the results were undeniable. If you have a goal you want to achieve, focus on taking the steps required to achieve that goal rather than visualizing yourself attaining that goal.

Even though Lebron visualized himself winning the championship he couldn't predict the challenges of securing the trophy, including playing in *The Bubble*, a confined arena, because of COVID-19. Don't let your visions distract you. The purpose of visualization is to have a North Star. It's something that will keep you heading in the right direction. Your vision is an imaginary representation of your goal. On the other hand, the creative journey is filled with unforeseen complications, new ideas, and influences. Don't try to win a specific goal; try to become a winner by focusing on the journey.

The amount of work you put into your process will determine your results. The formula for creative success is Process x Effort = Results. Focus on the process of perfectly laying down ten bricks daily and, in a matter of time, you will single-handedly build a mansion. Rate yourself based on your effort. Be happier when your best effort results in defeat than when a weak effort results in victory. Move with diligence instead of pushing for the rewards. The finish line will arrive.

Key of Environment

"To have a sacred place is an absolute necessity for anybody today. You must have a room or a certain hour of the day or so, where you do not know who your friends are, you don't know what you owe anybody or what they owe you. This is a place where you can simply experience and bring forth what you are and what you might be."—Joseph Campbell

JACOB COLLIER

Jacob Collier is a once-in-a-generation musical phenomenon. Collier's impressive harmonic composition, layering technology, and vast knowledge of music match his infectious energy and passion for his craft. He gained fame on YouTube as a teenager. He showcased his incredible musical abilities through complex compositions and engaged his fans by explaining the intricacies of classic songs. He did all of this from the comfort of his music room in Finchley.

In 2020, Jacob Collier's popularity exploded. He performed an impressive NPR Tiny Desk concert featuring six versions of himself playing various instruments, singing, and talking to each other over the internet. He also wowed audiences with a similar performance on a Jimmy Kimmel show appearance where three versions of himself popped up on a video call to perform his new single. What's particularly impressive is that Collier's musical genius resides in a special room previously used by his mother to give violin lessons. Now, the space houses his digital audio setup and an ever-growing collection of musical instruments.

When talking to NPR about recording music in his room, Jacob said, "That's what makes the homemade bedroom thing so 'characterful,' that you're feeding off your environment. That this is your world, you're in the world in which you're creating things, and you essentially end up describing the things around you. I think that's a very 'home-ly' and honest way of making music. I can't imagine making music in any other space."[23]

Jacob Collier is one of many examples of creative individuals with dedicated workspaces. Another is J.K. Rowling, the author famous for writing the *Harry Potter* series. She's known for having a dedicated space to work on her books in peace and solitude. She wrote much of the book in a café called The Elephant House, which she said had "the perfect atmosphere for writing." Georgia O'Keeffe, Thomas Edison, Frida Kahlo, and Ernest Hemingway are a handful of other creative geniuses who had dedicated creative workspaces, too.

IT'S MORE THAN A ROOM

In his YouTube channel, Jacob Collier's workspace is tidy and organized. This observation brings up an important point: a creative space is more than just the physical location and tools. It's also about how everything in your area relates to each other. Is it messy or clean? How does it make you feel when you enter your space? Does it inspire

---

[23] King, J. (2016, July 11). With "in my room," jazz phenom Jacob Collier is bringing jubilation back. NPR. https://www.npr.org/sections/therecord/2016/07/11/4852 61328/with-in-my-room-jazz-phenom-jacob-collier-is-bringing-jubilation-back

you to do something daring?

Psychologist Sabine Kastner wanted to answer these questions and investigate the myth of the disorganized genius. Despite what some famously messy creative thinkers like Albert Einstein and Steve Jobs believed, Kastner found that clutter depletes our mental resources by competing for attention with the problem we're trying to solve. The question popped into her head while she walked across a street and realized her mind strictly focused on one thing in her environment. She realized that nobody had investigated what captures our attention and what doesn't.

Kastner faced a problem in her research: how could she replicate the chaotic mess of real life in a sterile lab? Previously, scientists used simple standard shapes to measure the brain's response to things competing for attention. She knew this approach didn't accurately portray the messiness of real life, so Kastner took a different approach. Instead, she showed participants pictures of real-life scenes. She asked them to focus on a car or pick out a person from the scene. While doing this task, an MRI machine scanned their brain for patterns.

The MRI results showed that our brains are experts at finding very specific things. Once participants knew what they were looking for, they subconsciously ignored the other details in the scene and nearly erased the context. For example, when Kastner told participants to focus on cars, they saw outlines of car shapes in the entire image and blocked out anything that didn't fit their memories of cars. Then she took it a step further. When Kastner introduced random objects, it distracted the majority of the participants and interfered with their pattern recognition. Dr. Kastner concluded that when you're thinking deeply, your brain experiences a push towards the solution of whatever problem you are working on and a pull away from the solution by everything else competing for your attention.[24] This finding indicates our brains don't work well with clutter when trying to solve a complex problem.

THE UNIVERSAL CREATIVE WORKSPACE

If you're struggling to create a creative space or need to be creative but you're far from your dedicated space, here's a hack: many creative geniuses spend a lot of time outside.

One example is the well-known painter, Vincent van Gogh. He believed that spending time in nature was essential for his creative process for three main reasons:

1. Nature provided endless inspiration for his art. The natural world's colors, textures, and forms inspired his paintings.
2. Being in nature cleared his mind and allowed creativity to flow. He spent hours outdoors sketching and painting and felt that the peace and solitude of nature allowed him to focus on his art without distractions.
3. He believed that nature had a calming and grounding effect on him, which helped him stay focused and creative. He felt that spending time in nature balanced his mood and emotions and allowed him to create his best work.

You can benefit from creating in nature, too. A study by the University of Melbourne in Australia found that students who studied in a room with natural elements, like plants, performed better on concentration

---

[24] Seidl-Rathkopf, Katharina N., Nicholas B. Turk-Browne, and Sabine Kastner. 2015. "Automatic Guidance of Attention during Real-World Visual Search." Attention, Perception, & Psychophysics 77 (6): 1881–95. https://doi.org/10.3758/s13414-015-0903-8.

and memory tests than students who studied in a room without natural elements. Working outside or incorporating natural elements into your indoor workspace can improve concentration and cognitive function.[25]

YOUR SPACE

Now that you've learned how other creative people use their environment to their advantage, it's time to apply this to your workspace.

Make sure your space is comfortable and conducive to concentration. Tweak it by decluttering your desk, improving the lighting, or adjusting the temperature. Experiment with the colors and decor of your space because they will impact your creativity. For example, using colors like blue or green promotes creative thinking. Incorporate natural elements like a plant, a picture of a natural scene, or even a window with an outdoor view. Also, ensure your space is conducive to relaxation because creativity significantly improves when you relax your mind. Consider including elements like a comfortable chair or calming music.

Keep in mind that everyone is different, so what works for one person may not work for another. Experiment with various elements and see what helps you be the most creative. Use the suggestions in this key for direction, but remember, creating an environment that enhances your creativity is a personal process. It will take trial and error to find what works best for you. Create a space where unleashing your creative potential feels most natural.

---

[25] Vella-Brodrick, Dianne A., and Krystyna Gilowska. 2022. "Effects of Nature (Greenspace) on Cognitive Functioning in School Children and Adolescents: A Systematic Review." Educational Psychology Review 34 (March). https://doi.org/10.1007/s10648-022-09658-5.

Key of Production

"Draw the art you want to see, start the business you want to run, play the music you want to hear, write the books you want to read, build the products you want to use – do the work you want to see done."—Austin Kleon

CONSUMING VS CREATING

What did Leonardo da Vinci and Albert Einstein have in common? They both left behind more for the world than they took from the world.

People remember Leonardo da Vinci for his impressive achievements in a wide range of fields, including art, science, engineering, and more. His notebooks demonstrate his incredible creativity and drive to create and innovate. They contain thousands of pages of his observations, ideas, and designs.

Similarly, Albert Einstein was best known for his theory of relativity, but all of his discoveries have profoundly impacted science and technology. In addition to his scientific work, he was an accomplished violinist and advocated for social justice. He was a prolific writer and published hundreds of papers and articles on a wide range of topics.

Consuming is the act of taking in information. You consume when listening to music, appreciating art, scrolling through social media, watching your favorite TV shows, and reading books. Creating is the act of releasing information. You create when playing music, painting on a canvas, releasing content on TikTok, filming videos, and writing a book. What you create is the mark you leave behind on this world.

Most people consume while creators are the minority. Learn how to have balance. Don't spend too much time embodying a consumer who spends all of their time admiring the few creators who are releasing their ideas. Creative geniuses are visionaries actively transforming their thoughts into reality. They are constantly aware that nobody praises them for the ideas trapped inside their minds. They are the movers and shakers of the world because they cycle between consuming and releasing their inspiration. There's balance.

PRIORITIZE PRODUCING

Do not completely stop consuming. Consuming helps improve the things you create by giving you fresh knowledge and inspiration to pull from. Instead, consume at a level that allows your creativity to grow.

Consuming should blend seamlessly into your creative journey. The primary purpose of education is not to acquire knowledge but to utilize what you learn. Yet, a lot of creative people practice the opposite. Over-consumers learn a lot but lack something to show for it. Instead of practicing your craft, it's easy to get wrapped up in studying it. Don't fall into that trap. Prioritize producing. Every second you spend consuming should clash with an internal drive pulling you to create. Become a producer first and a consumer second. I know it's not easy, but it's necessary.

DYING IDEAS

Motivational speaker Les Brown said, "The graveyard is the richest place on earth because it is here that you will find all the hopes and dreams that were never fulfilled, the books that were never written, the songs that were never sung, the inventions that were never shared, the cures that were never discovered, all because someone was too afraid to take that first step, keep with the problem, or determined to carry out their dream."

Don't let your ideas lay dormant. You have an important choice to make. Are you going to be a consumer or a creator? In ten years, do you want to have a successful YouTube channel, published books, art shows, and music albums? Or do you want to be the person who stays in the loop of the latest TV shows, songs, and news? Do you want to be a part of pop culture, or do you want to keep up with it? Remember, you can't change the world from the sidelines.

* * *

Did any of these keys spark an interesting thought?
Share it with me at WorldOfCreatives.com

Key of Cross-fertilization

"To know everything is to know nothing, but to know something about everything is to have some idea of what everything is about."—Unknown

LEONARDO DA VINCI

Leonardo da Vinci was my childhood inspiration. I aspired to be like him. The more I researched him, the more I was in awe of his mind. His ideas were so ahead of his time that conspiracy theorists believe he's a time traveler.

You may know him for painting the *Mona Lisa* and *The Last Supper*, some of the world's most famous art, but he's more than an artist. Leonardo da Vinci is the quintessential Renaissance Man. The term "Renaissance Man" originated during the Renaissance period in Europe when scholars, artists, and thinkers explored a range of disciplines. The term became popular because Leonardo excelled in painting, sculpture, mathematics, engineering, anatomy, music, and more. He was a rare breed of creative genius. Most creators are either intellectually deep in one topic or shallow in many topics. Leonardo da Vinci went deep into many topics.

As an artist, he pioneered oil painting. He was the first artist to use perspective, chiaroscuro, contrapposto, sfumato, and many other painting techniques. He didn't only create art. He elevated it.

In the realm of engineering, Leonardo da Vinci was a visionary. He drafted plans for a diverse range of inventions, including a helicopter, a parachute, folding furniture, automated musical instruments, a water-powered alarm clock, the bicycle, an extendable ladder, an armored tank, a machine gun, a guided missile, a submarine, and many more. But his most significant contribution to engineering wasn't any of his inventions. It was his concept of automation. He saw the potential for machines to alleviate human labor and enhance productivity long before the Industrial Revolution.

Da Vinci was also a trailblazer in anatomy and botany. He dissected human bodies and made detailed drawings, pioneering modern comparative anatomy. In botany, he was the first to note the relationship between a tree's age and the number of rings in its trunk.

And here's the thing: all of these achievements happened in the 1400s. Leonardo da Vinci's curious mind noted observations that predated many discoveries by Copernicus, Galileo, Newton, and Darwin.

40 years before Copernicus proposed that the Sun is the center of the solar system and that the planets circle the Sun, Da Vinci noted, "The sun does not move…The earth is not in the center of the circle of the sun, nor in the center of the universe."

60 years before Galileo, he suggested that "a large magnifying lens" should be employed to study space.

200 years before Newton's theory of gravitation, Leonardo wrote, "Every weight tends to fall towards the center by the shortest possible way…every heavy substance presses downward, and cannot be upheld perpetually, the whole earth must become spherical."

400 years before Darwin, da Vinci noted that man does not vary from animals except in what is accidental. He also observed geotropism, the gravitational attraction of the earth on some plants, and heliotropism,

the attraction of plants toward the sun.[26]

These are all just a few of his contributions to humanity. Leonardo da Vinci's ideas shaped the world we live in. He was ahead of his time and deserved the title Renaissance Man.

INCREASING YOUR CHANCES OF WINNING A NOBEL PEACE PRIZE

In 2008, a team of researchers conducted a study on how creativity influences other fields. They compared Nobel Prize-winning scientists from 1901 to 2005 with other expert scientists of their time. They found that Nobel Prize scientists were more likely to have a hobby in the arts than their less accomplished colleagues. The table below summarizes this correlation:

---

26 Gelb, Michael J. 2009. How to Think like Leonardo Da Vinci. [S.I.]: Random House Publishing Group.

Odds of Nobel Prize winners being involved in the hobby relative to the average scientist	Creative hobby
2x more likely	Music hobby (playing an instrument, composing, conducting)
7x more likely	Fine Art hobby (painting, sculpting, printmaking)
7.5x more likely	Crafting hobby (mechanics, woodworking, electronics, glassblowing)
12x more likely	Writing hobby (poetry, plays, novels, stories, essays, books)
22x more likely	Performing Arts hobby (actor, dancer, magician)

Yes, you read that correctly. Nobel Prize winners were 2x more likely to have a music hobby than the average scientist. 7x more likely to have a Fine Art or Crafting hobby, 12x more likely to have a writing hobby, and a whopping 22x more likely to have a performing arts hobby like acting, dancing, or even being a magician.[27]

This is not limited to science. Creativity researchers often see this phenomenon when observing how people succeed in multiple areas. This is one of the core benefits of creativity. It's an unfair advantage you can apply in every aspect of your life. Once mastered, it's like

---

[27] RootBernstein, Robert, Lindsay Allen, Leighanna Beach, Ragini Bhadula, Justin Fast, Chelsea Hosey, Benjamin Kremkow, et al. 2008. "Arts Foster Scientific Success: Avocations of Nobel, National Academy, Royal Society, and Sigma Xi Members." Journal of Psychology of Science and Technology 1 (October): 51–63. https://doi.or g/10.1891/19397054.1.2.51.

carrying a gun to a knife fight in another field.

THE BLEND

Science and art are two ends on the spectrum of creativity. When we engage in science, we use our creativity to gather facts in hopes to make sense of the world. It's the intricate dance of hypothesis, experimentation, and validation that brings us closer to truth. On the other hand, art is a world of make-believe where our imagination runs wild. This is where we harness the ability to create things that we've never seen before, molding the nonexistent into tangible forms. The space between science and art is filled with an abundance of creative potential.

A NAIVE EXPERT

One creative way to generate new ideas is to seek out and talk to a naïve expert. A naïve expert is someone who is intelligent and knowledgeable, but not an expert in your specific field. By exchanging ideas and discussing challenges with a naïve expert, you can gain new perspectives and insights that may not be available to you if you only talk to experts in your field. The beauty of talking to a naïve expert is that they are skilled at coming up with creative solutions, but they are not limited by the same conventions, habits, and patterns of thinking that you may have. Take advantage of this opportunity to expand your thinking and see where it takes you. Even if the conversation doesn't directly solve your problem, it will likely spark new ideas and inspire you to think in new ways.

PARADOX OF CREATIVE EXPERTISE

Deep subject-matter expertise is essential for creative mastery, but it can also be restrictive. When you first started in your creative field, ideas likely flowed freely until you eventually gained more expertise. Over time, that flow can start to slow down or even stop. This is a common problem for many creators.

Disney executive Duncan Wardle addressed this issue in a TED Talk about the "theory of creativity."[28] He used a simple experiment to illustrate how deep expertise hinders creativity. He gathered architects and a Chinese chef and asked them to sketch a house. The architects' drawings were all similar, but the chef's sketch was the most creative. It was a mixture of the places around China where he grew up and, unsurprisingly, food. His lack of expertise freed his mind to combine various experiences to create something unique.

The problem with strictly drawing inspiration from deep expertise is that it only takes you down familiar paths. Experts are so deeply entrenched in their thought patterns that it is unlikely for them to mentally venture out into the wild even though non-experts can. These creative barriers are why many music artists peak early in their careers. Like the architects in the previous experiment, they get mentally trapped inside the nuances of their craft. Their creativity becomes pigeonholed. Non-experts have an advantage in coming up with unique ideas because they don't have knowledge that forces limiting beliefs. Use this to your advantage by creating outside what you usually pursue. You never know what fields you can dominate when your skills transfer over. And the things you learn elsewhere will, in turn, improve your main craft.

---

[28] Wardle, Duncan. n.d. "The Theory of Creativity." www.ted.com. https://www.ted.com/talks/duncan_wardle_the_theory_of_creativity.

MONA LISA

An excellent example of combining disciplines is Leonardo da Vinci's *Mona Lisa* painting. Her smile is legendary because sometimes she looks like she's smiling, and other times she isn't. But did you know that Leonardo da Vinci intentionally painted her that way?

When Leonardo was dissecting the human eye, he noted that light rays do not come to a single point in the eye but instead hit the entire area of the retina. That was the key to her smile. The smile comes and goes because of how our visual system is designed, not because the expression is ambiguous. After all his anatomy research was complete, he jotted down the initial sketch of Mona Lisa's smile, his idea of a perfect smile that would fool our eyes for centuries to come.

Using this sketch, Leonardo invented a painting technique called sfumato and chiaroscuro to tackle this feat. Using sfumato, he painted thin translucent layers of brushstrokes applied over many years, making sure there weren't any lines visible to the naked eye. This allows us to look at a painting using depth of field—the way our eyes work. Using chiaroscuro, he contrasted shades of light and dark to create the illusions of a 3D form. All of this required so many thin layers of paint that many of the layers faded away over time. The Mona Lisa we see today is vastly different from the Mona Lisa back then. For example, Giorgio Vasari, an Italian Renaissance Master, noted the exceptional realism of Mona Lisa's eyebrows. Yet, if you look at the painting today, you will see that she doesn't have any eyebrows. They both faded away, lost in time.

Leonardo painted the Mona Lisa at 60 years old, a few years before he passed away. This artwork was the only painting he traveled with, along with his notebooks of research and inventions. When you're looking at the Mona Lisa, you're looking at more than a portrait; you're looking at the accumulated knowledge of a genius who blended art and science to create a magical work of art.

MASTER ALL ALL

I don't agree with the phrase, "A Jack of all trades is a master of none, but oftentimes better than a master of one." A Jack of all trades can be a master of one or even a master of few. It's seen in the lives of many of history's greatest creators. Salvador Dali expanded beyond painting, venturing into realms like jewelry, clothing design, and crafts. He dabbled in other fields to improve his main focus, his dreamy painting. Creative geniuses use what they learn from pursuing mastery in other fields to help them master their main field. Along the way some creators ended up being masters of many. For example, Michelangelo was a well-rounded artist who not only etched the marbled masterpiece The David, but also painted one of the most technically advanced paintings on the Sistine Chapel's massive walls and ceilings.

CROSS-FERTILIZATION: BORROWING FROM ANALOGOUS FIELDS

Cross-fertilization is the process of sharing ideas or techniques between different fields, disciplines, or industries to stimulate innovation and creativity. This can involve borrowing ideas from analogous fields or collaborating with people from diverse backgrounds. The goal of cross-fertilization is to combine different perspectives and knowledge to generate new and creative solutions. This is not possible by working within a single field. You have to expand into other disciplines.

Innovative businesses use cross-fertilization to their advantage. For example, 3M, a well-known American conglomerate that produces over 60,000 products under several brands, worked with a theater make-up expert to develop products and methods that reduce skin infections after surgery.

The Harvard Business Review studied the benefits of cross-fertilization. They recruited carpenters, inline skaters, and roofers and asked them to brainstorm ideas for improving the safety gear used in their own field. Then, they asked them to suggest the same for the other two fields. The researchers found that each group thought of better ideas for domains other than their own. In fact, the more different the two fields were from each other, the more creative the participant became.

To unlock your creative potential, give yourself the freedom to explore other hobbies without pursuing mastery. This can be difficult for ambitious creators, but it is essential. Prioritize practice over perfection. Each hobby will influence the other in ways that are undetectable by the conscious mind.

Key of Children

"The creative adult is the child who survived."—Ursula LeGuin

BASQUIAT

Jean-Michel Basquiat died in 1988 at the young age of twenty-seven after creating over 1500 drawings and 600 paintings. Basquiat was a mixture of creative genius and rebellious teenager. He was hyper-aware of social issues that affected his generation. He was intelligent enough to understand that art had to be dealt with like a business to be successful, but he lacked the maturity to find balance in his personal life. He socialized with the elite of the art world but was constantly at war with himself, loving the labels society placed on him and then loathing them. His "wild child" persona pleased him and yet also repulsed him. Even his art was a constant dichotomy of themes depicting "wealth vs poverty, segregation vs integration, and inner vs outer experiences."[29]

Basquiat was aware of the power of maintaining a childlike mindset. In an interview with Vanity Fair he said, "I want to make paintings that look as if they were made by a child." His journey is an example

---

[29] "Jean-Michel Basquiat." n.d. Dellasposa. https://www.dellasposa.com/artists/48-jean-michel-basquiat/.

of how an intellectual creator's passion for illuminating social and political injustices can simultaneously be deeply connected to their inner child. His art expresses adult themes in a way that appears simplistic and relatable, yet complex and disturbing. He managed to retain his freedom by intentionally showing an energy of unrestrained and manic urgency in his art.

STAGES OF ARTISTIC DEVELOPMENT

When I think about kids being creative, I think about blankets stretched over chairs in the living room to create forts and mystical lands. I think about them tying a towel around their neck, spreading their arms out, and imagining themselves soaring thousands of feet in the air. They use art supplies to create colorful drawings backed by fantastical stories. It's undeniable that children are creative, but it's also clear that the percentage of creative kids is drastically higher than the percentage of creative adults. When I asked a room filled with preschoolers, "Raise your hand if you're creative," the majority of them enthusiastically raised their hands. When I asked a room of adults, a few reluctantly raised their hands.

The reason this happens lies in Dr. Viktor Lowenfeld's stages of artistic development. In 1947, he posed that there are six stages of artistic development that every child goes through from age 1 to 16, and that these stages can be observed in the art they create.[30] Let's briefly go over the six stages:

---

[30] Viktor Lowenfeld, and W Lambert Brittain. 1987. Creative and Mental Growth. New York, N.Y.: Collier Books.

Stage 1: Scribble Stage (1 – 3 years old)

Children draw simple lines to experience the movements. They may name or tell stories about their scribbles.

Stage 2: Preschematic Stage (3 – 4 years old)

Children start to communicate through their drawings by developing their schema, the visual identity of their drawings. Their scribbles describe people or objects important to them scattered around the paper.

Stage 3: The Schematic Stage (5 – 6 years old)

Children in this stage show a better understanding of space by placing objects on the ground instead of floating and having a clear separation between the ground and sky. Objects of greater importance, like their parents, are drawn larger than less important objects, like their house.

Stage 4: The Dawning Realism (7 – 9 years old)

Children in this stage attempt to draw more realistic with three dimensional techniques and shading using multiple colors. For the first time in their life, they become aware of their lack of ability to draw objects exactly as they appear in real life, so they become critical of their own work.

Stage 5: The Pseudo-Realistic Stage (10 – 13 years old)

In the previous stages, children cared most about the process of creating art. Now, in this stage, they care more about the end result. At this stage the art can be based on how they feel about things they experience in their life. Most children stop drawing at this stage because they become frustrated that their art doesn't look like real life.

Stage 6: The Decision Stage (13 – 16 years old)

The few children that reach this stage typically continue identifying as an artist for the rest of their life. They continue to develop their creative minds because they retain the belief that art is an activity without merit.

Thus, children's art starts off as playful, joyful, and unconcerned with the expectations of representing life as it is. They're simply expressing themself. By middle-childhood, their drawings become more stereotypical as they focus on the rules of realistic representation. The biggest drop off of creativity happens in the transition from the Pseudo-Realistic Stage to the Decision Stage. Children's self criticism about art hinders them from embracing the creative process and causes them to fear the judgment of their final works of art. Without deep encouragement from their peers and family to push through, they let go of creativity and start to view it as a trait a few other people have and they don't possess.

CREATIVITY IS NOT LEARNED, IT'S UNLEARNED.

In the most watched TED Talk called "Do schools kill creativity?" Sir Ken Robinson explained that "we don't grow into creativity, we grow out of it." Every child develops creatively the same way they progress through the stages of artistic development. Children start life fearlessly observing the world with a curious mind to express novel ideas. As they grow older, society dims their light and pushes them into conventional thinking.

Repetitive learning and standardized testing in schools stifle children's creativity. Their focus on memorization and test-taking is the opposite of playtime. When kids engage extensively in pretend play, they are exercising the crucial imaginative thinking that helps them develop the creative skills they need as adults. Play, in all forms, is how humans grow to understand the world. Yet, rather than prioritizing play, schools smother kid's creative potential.

Extrinsic motivation is also another way society blocks creativity in both children and adults. When we're focused on external rewards like grades or paychecks, we're less likely to take risks and pursue novel ideas. Instead of focusing on external rewards, schools and the workplace should encourage intrinsic motivation and allow people to explore their interests and passions for the sake of learning and personal growth.

Another factor that hinders creativity in kids is adult's focus on obedience. Creativity requires taking social risks. Creative people generate novel ideas regardless of how the rest of the world thinks. In fact, creativity is most strongly associated with the willingness to challenge norms, which can be an ostracizing experience. When adults focus heavily on obedience and conformity, they may limit children's ability to think creatively and take risks. Instead, we should encourage children to safely challenge norms and explore new ideas, even if they may be met with resistance or rejection.

NURTURING CREATIVITY

Creativity is my passion, and frankly, it's all I know. I grew up in an environment that celebrated creativity. My father, Cecil Walker, was a chef and a crafty engineer, and my mother, Dian Walker, was a poet and teacher. My sister, Alexa, was a makeup artist. My closest childhood friends were passionate about film, acting, and music. My wife, Ife, is an artist and chef; coincidentally, her name means "Lover of Art." I also had the pleasure of growing up with a creative genius, one of my biggest influences, my older brother Omar aka "Major 7." I was honored to witness him go from a toddler punching keys on a toy piano to creating music for social icons like Rick Ross, Jay-Z, Rihanna, Future, and the like. It takes a village to raise a child and my village overflowed with creativity.

My formative years were immersed in inspiration. My community embraced all my questions about the world with open arms. They set me free to explore nature and various forms of creativity. Experimentation was encouraged, causing the line between failure and success to fade away. Pursuing my curiosity became the cornerstone of my creative journey.

I played the tenor saxophone, piano, and drums in my adolescence. Each instrument revealed a new facet of expression, teaching me that creativity is the language that transcends words.

My dad built a science lab for me in my basement, where I tinkered daily. From concocting mysterious potions to observing the intricate dance of chemical reactions, I realized that creativity flowed through the fabric of every field, from the arts to sciences.

When I wanted to be a ninja, I trained in ninjutsu. When I wanted to express myself through clothes, I modeled in fashion shows. When I wanted to be on stage, I performed magic tricks, poetry, spoken word, and plays. When I wanted to see a story on the big screen, I filmed and edited short films with my friends.

At fourteen years old, I studied various art forms in Italy, and a year later, I spent eight weeks apprenticing under master artists with a group of talented peers. I went on to win over fifty art contests in high school, locally, statewide, and internationally.

Years later, in 2021, ABC featured me on their tv show Shark Tank for creating an online art education business called Sparketh that has taught over 30,000 kids art in over 100 countries.

I wrote *Create or Die: 48 Keys of Creativity* out of passion. I've seen how creativity has impacted my life and the lives of people around me. Simply put: I have been a lifelong fan of creativity. My upbringing was filled with it. I started studying creativity because I want to understand how to continue unleashing my creativity throughout adulthood. My goal with this book is to teach you everything I discovered along my journey.

BABY GENIUSES

In 1968, George Land and Beth Jarman devised a creativity test for NASA to help select innovative engineers and scientists.[31] The test was to look at a problem and come up with new, different, innovative ideas. The test worked extremely well at identifying creative geniuses that could look at a problem and come up with innovative solutions. They decided to use the same test on five-year olds.

The results were astounding. 98% of 5 year olds scored at the "Genius Level" while only 2% of adults did. To show how creativity

---

[31] TEDx Talks. 2011. "TEDxTucson George Land the Failure of Success." YouTube. https://www.youtube.com/watch?v=ZfKMq-rYtnc.

is masked overtime, they retested the same participants years later. When they were 10 years old only 30% scored at the "Genius Level" and when they were 15 years olds it was only 12%.

We come into this world as natural creative geniuses. Creativity is not learned, it's unlearned.

A POEM TO ART

I feel like I've known you my whole life.
Your warm presence always felt so right,
Embraced by your security,
I finally felt free to be me.
You injected life in my ideas, as odd as they could be,
Displaying them proudly for the world to see,
You sparked my curiosity like a moon shining at night,
Overpowering my darkest thoughts with light.
I was lost at sea struggling to fight my waves within.
I was drowning in emotions when you taught me how to swim.
I'll never erase the mark you left on my life.
You added color to a world that felt black and white.
Yet, through all that you did for me, I drifted away.
They said "real life" is a game and I have to leave you to play.
Then suddenly you were taken, and my whole world was shaken.
"What do you mean that's unimportant? Sir, you must be
mistaken."
Honestly, I didn't understand,
But I trusted them and stuck to their plan.
I stood in those lines. I passed those tests.
I got that job, but now I'm just stressed.
And in a world of distractions, where everyone's average,
It's hard to express myself while feeling accepted.

Sometimes when I close my eyes to see, how vast my mind can
truly be,
I hear your whisper deep, deep down inside of me.
- A Poem to Art
by Dwayne Walker

There's a tug-of-war happening inside of us. A battle between who we are and who the world expects us to be. In chasing society's view on success and our place in this world, we often leave behind the vibrant colors of our true self, the parts that thrived in our childhood. Even when drowned out by life's noise, the whisper of our creative spirit echoes, waiting to be heard once more. It lingers in our choices, dreams, and hearts. The bravest thing you can do is fight for your authenticity. By finding yourself, you will find all the answers you seek.

TAPPING INTO YOUR INNER CHILD

The good news is your creativity didn't go away. It's just tucked away. By tapping into the inner child you return to a previous time when your life was much freer. As adults, you lose the childhood qualities of curiosity and imagination, you fear for the unknown and the future outcomes you can't control. This leads to less risk-taking, sticking to familiar ways of thinking and doing, and losing the spark that ignites the passion and enthusiasm to explore, reinvent, and create.

Like Picasso once said, "Every child is an artist. The problem is how to remain an artist once we grow up." Children display raw emotions. They are resilient, fearlessly curious, present, unrestricted by consequences, imaginative, and not bound by the conformity and the pressures of adulthood. When you reconnect with these qualities, you unlock your inner child. When you unlock your inner child, you unlock your creative spirit. This is the number one goal you must pursue as a creator.

Key of Failure

"Have no fear of perfection. You will never reach it."—Salvador Dali

JK ROWLING

As an adult, I'm still in awe at the magical world, plot, and characters in *Harry Potter*. The *Harry Potter* franchise has generated an estimated revenue of over $25 billion worldwide. JK Rowling, the author behind the iconic series, knows a thing or two about failure. In fact, she credits her struggles as the driving force behind her massive success as a writer. Not only did she overcome the challenges of being an unemployed, newly divorced, young single parent, but she learned from it.

In 2008, Rowling gave an acceptance speech at Harvard.[32] She shared her insights as a wise, motivated, and self-determined person who faced the difficulties of balancing her own ambitions with the limitations others placed on her. She wanted to be a writer, but her parents didn't believe she could find success in that career path. But Rowling proved them wrong, and she did it all through hard work,

---

[32] "J.K. Rowling Speaks at Harvard Commencement." 2011. YouTube Video. YouTube. https://www.youtube.com/watch?v=wHGqp8lz36c.

determination, and a willingness to learn from her failures.

Shortly after graduation, the birth of her child, and a short-lived marriage, she experienced firsthand "the fear, depression, stress, humiliation, and hardships" that poverty brings. At rock bottom, she realized that she feared failure more than poverty. This motivated her to overshadow her fear of failure by her desire to succeed.

"Why do I talk about the benefits of failure?" she said. "Simply because failure meant a stripping away of the inessential. I stopped pretending to myself that I was anything other than what I was, and began to direct all my energy into finishing the only work that mattered to me. Had I succeeded in anything else, I might never have found the determination to succeed in the one area where I believed I truly belonged. I was set free because my greatest fear had been realized and I was still alive."

The process was liberating. During her speech, she made a statement that sums up the fear of failure in a nutshell. She said, "It is impossible to live without failing at something unless you live so cautiously that you might as well not have lived at all—in which case, you fail by default."

FEAR OF FAILURE

As a creative person, there's nothing scarier than staring down a blank canvas. You start asking yourself all sorts of questions: What am I going to create? Am I going to mess this up? Will people like it? Did I bite off more than I can chew?

Fear of failure is a common issue for creative types. It can stem from basic self-doubt and build up to doubts about the success of your career. After all, creativity is an expression of self, and when others judge your work, it can feel like a personal attack. Every time you share your ideas with the world, you open yourself up to the possibility of negative criticism.

And when it comes to our careers, we often feel pressure to succeed because we think failure reflects poorly on our creative reputation. Simply put, creators fear failure because of the judgment of others. The scary thing about judgment is how influential it can be if you believe it. Creative people who struggle with self-doubt and may worry that their ideas aren't good enough or that they're not capable of creating successful work.

THE PYGMALION EFFECT

Kanye once said, "I always feel like I can do anything. That's the main thing people are controlled by. Their perception of themselves. They're slowed down by their perceptions of themselves. If you're taught you can't do anything you won't do anything. I was taught I can do anything." The Pygmalion Effect, also known as the Rosenthal Effect, is a phenomenon that shows how the expectations of others can significantly impact an individual's performance.[33] This was accidentally discovered with a group of elementary school students. First, teachers tested the kids and then accidentally placed the lowest-scorers in advanced classes and the highest-scorers in the lower classes. Both the students and teachers believed they were supposed to be in those classes.

Six months went by before they realized the mistake that had been made, but the results were shocking. The students who were originally underperforming actually outperformed the other classroom of academically stronger students in every measure. This has two key takeaways: other people's beliefs about us influence their actions

---

[33] The Decision Lab. n.d. "The Pygmalion Effect - the Decision Lab." The Decision Lab. https://thedecisionlab.com/biases/the-pygmalion-effect.

towards us, and their actions towards us influence and reinforce our beliefs about ourselves.

The Pygmalion Effect is a self-fulfilling prophecy. It proves that we rise or fall to the expectations placed upon us by the people we surround ourselves with. Other people's judgment about your creativity can cause you to doubt yourself and fuel your fear of failure if you don't intentionally block it.

There's a chance that you've already fallen into this psychological trap. But there's still hope. Sometimes you have to fight fire with fire, and that's where Atkinson's theory of achievement motivation comes into play.

ATKINSON'S THEORY OF ACHIEVEMENT MOTIVATION

How do some creators overcome fear and reach high levels of creative success? That's what Atkinson's theory of achievement motivation tries to explain. Atkinson says that achievement-motivation is a mix of things, but mainly it's an individual's personal need for achievement—the desire to succeed and excel at tasks and activities. This need for achievement can be strong or weak, depending on someone's beliefs about themselves. According to this psychological theory, people who are more achievement-motivated tend to be more focused on their goals, work harder to reach them, and aren't afraid to face obstacles or setbacks.[34]

You can leverage this theory to overcome your fear of failure. Start by dedicating time to figuring out what motivates you. Dig deep. Then once you figure it out, fight your fear of failure with what motivates

---

[34] "Achievement Motivation." 2020. Www.youtube.com. November 13, 2020. https://www.youtube.com/watch?v=dA5xUs3zdYs.

you the most. In JK Rowlings' case, hitting rock bottom and having something to prove was her motivation.

According to Atkinson's theory of achievement motivation, people who are high in achievement motivation tend to be more open to taking risks and trying new things, because they have the fuel required to succeed and reach their goals. This willingness to take risks and embrace challenges can be a huge boost for your creativity, as it allows you to explore new ideas and approaches, and to be more daring in your creative endeavors.

Atkinson's theory also suggests that people who are high in achievement motivation tend to have more self-confidence and feel more in control of their lives and destinies. This self-confidence will help you believe in your creative abilities and pursue challenging projects with a sense of purpose and direction.

A SELF-LOVING IDEA

"Lean into your strengths. Compensate for your weaknesses." This quote is common advice, but when I hear it, I can't help but disagree.

I used to feel like there were two halves of me. On one side, there's grit, creativity, passion, curiosity, and empathy. I called these strengths. On the other side was unorganized, people-pleasing, obsessiveness, overly optimistic, and overthinking. I called these weaknesses.

I felt self-aware. In some scenarios, my strengths gave me confidence. I felt on top of the world. On the contrary, I tried to avoid moments that revealed my weaknesses—moments when I felt inadequate.

I've since questioned the concept of "strengths and weaknesses," and I'm starting to break out of its box. I found myself trapped in its illusion, and you might be, too.

To love yourself more, I challenge you to embrace your weaknesses just as much as you embrace your strengths because here's my newfound truth: Weaknesses are strengths applied in the wrong areas.

Impatience is imperative in fast-paced environments where quick decision-making is crucial, such as an emergency response. Perfectionism isn't paralyzing in meticulous fields like graphic design, quality assurance, or scientific research. Procrastination is a superpower when it's time to execute under pressure. Sensitivity breeds deeper connections. Shyness breeds keen observation. Impulsiveness breeds spontaneous lives.

Every quality about you is beautiful. This one idea can unlock more self-love, happiness, and success. I hope it reframes your perspective a bit. Reflect on your weaknesses, and reimagine them as untapped strengths. Redirect their energy towards areas where they serve you best. Reframe. Reflect. Redirect.

EMBRACING YOUR FEAR OF FAILURE

Richard Allen Garriott is a pioneering video game developer and entrepreneur, celebrated for his creation of the Ultima series and his contributions to spaceflight. He attributed much of his ability to change the world to his willingness to fail in the face of new opportunities. In his memoir *Explore/Create*, he wrote:

"I do buy into the adage that luck is the intersection of preparation and opportunity. Opportunities parade past all of us all the time. The key is that you must be paying attention to see them, you must be willing to take risks, you must expose yourself to the possibility of massive failure and you must believe in what you are doing so much that you do it anyway. This attitude has enabled me to help create and build two world-impacting industries: computer games and commercial spaceflight."[35]

Fear of failure is a natural emotion, but that fear can hold you back from achieving greatness in your creative endeavors. Here's how you combat this fear: First, identify the root cause of your fear. Think about times when you've failed in the past and how you dealt with it. Use that experience to pin your root fear against your root motivation. Because the truth is you're going to fail. You're going to succeed too, but you're going to experience a series of failures along the way. And that's okay. When you're fearless of failure, you take ownership of your successes and failures equally because both are viewed as opportunities to learn.

Failure allows you to reflect on what went wrong and identify areas for improvement. Yes, it's natural to feel disappointment or frustration, but it's important to reframe your perspective and see the situation as an opportunity to learn and grow. Use your failure to provide insight into what didn't work and help you understand what you need to do differently in the future. And as you reflect on your failure, it can help you become more self-aware. Use that insight to develop yourself and your ideas to solve your next creative challenge. Embrace failure as a chance to grow because each lesson is a step closer to unlocking your creative potential.

* * *

Did any of these keys spark an interesting thought?
Share it with me at WorldOfCreatives.com

---

[35] Garriott, R., & Fisher, D. (2017). Explore/create: My life in pursuit of New Frontiers, hidden worlds, and the creative spark. William Morrow.

Key of Action

"Procrastination is the thief of time."—Edward Young

CREATE

As creators, we tend to focus on the ideas we come up with rather than the work we produce. Yet, it is only through the act of creating that we receive recognition and praise. Unfortunately, it's easy to get caught up in the planning and analyzing phase, never taking the necessary action to bring their ideas to fruition.

There are countless cases of artists who paint for years without showing their artwork, singers who never release their music, and writers who never publish their books. The critical difference between these individuals and the most successful creators is their willingness to take action. That's how ideas come to life. Successful creators prefer to improve their creativity by adapting to challenges along their creative process rather than over-planning.

You can't predict every potential pitfall. Get started and use the act of creation to overcome challenges and refine your ideas. Embrace the power of action.

LAW OF ATTRACTION

Have you wondered how your thoughts and feelings impact the events and outcomes in your life? The law of attraction is a concept that's been around for centuries. It suggests that your thoughts can manifest experiences in your life. Whether or not you believe in the law of attraction, it's worth considering its core concept to pursue your creative desires because action plays a critical role.

The relationship between taking action and the law of attraction is simple. There are two parts to the law of attraction: thoughts and actions. Many people know about the power of positive thinking and how instrumental it is in reaching your goals. However, most people need to be aware of the second half of the equation: action. When you take action on your goals and desires, you show your commitment and belief in them, which can help attract people and opportunities to bring them closer to reality.

For example, perhaps you dream of starting a successful business selling handmade jewelry. In addition to focusing on positive thoughts and feelings about your business, you decide to take action to bring your dream closer to reality. This includes creating a website and social media presence, networking with other jewelry makers and industry professionals, and making your jewelry. By taking these actions, you allow opportunities to find you. People may become fans of your work and share it with their friends. Event organizers may reach out, offering booth space at their conventions. Other jewelers with larger followings may want to collaborate on a collection. All of which came about from action, not thinking.

Unpredictable opportunities present themselves to you when you move past the thinking stage. The possibilities are endless. So, if you want to make the most of the law of attraction, don't only focus on your thoughts. Take action, too.

WALT DISNEY

Walt Disney created some of the most iconic characters and films in history. Still, one of his most outstanding achievements was the creation of Disneyland. Hidden under Disneyland's iconic rise in popularity is a story of challenges, setbacks, and, ultimately, the power of taking action on an outlandish dream.

Walt Disney dreamed of building this theme park for years. Unlike most creatives, he decided to commit to making his idea a reality. After spending years creating every detail of the park, his vision still faced challenges like limited funding and skepticism. However, he remained determined and refused to let his idea sit idle.

Finally, after years of relentless hard work, Disneyland opened up to the public and was a massive hit. It was a first of its kind and set the standard for all theme parks to this day. Over the years, Disneyland has brought joy to millions of people worldwide. This story illustrates the importance of the Key of Action. It shows that when you choose to take action, even in the face of adversity, you can turn your most ambitious dreams into a reality.

TAKE IT NOW

A few years ago, I noticed my wife mixing oregano, parsley, and other herbs and spices into her dog's food. When I asked her why she was doing that, she told me about all the benefits different natural herbs and spices had for dogs. I wondered, "Would people buy a seasoning blend for dog food that boosted their health?". For most people, the steps to starting a business like this would be crafting a formula, finding a manufacturer, creating a professional logo, printing labels, you name it. I cut through all those steps. Instead, I photoshopped an image of an imaginary product, put it on a website, and promoted it as if it were a fully operational company. That day, I got over one hundred sales. I emailed each customer and said, "Unfortunately, we are out of stock. You can either get a refund now or wait until we restock for us to fulfill your order." All the customers opted to wait patiently as my wife and I hustled to bring this validated idea to life.

The best advice I received in college was from Christopher Hanks, the Founder & Executive Director of KSU's Entrepreneurship Center. In his lecture about creating a business, he wrote on the whiteboard in big, bold letters, "TAKE ACTION!". He went on to explain that taking action is the key to bringing anything to life. Your most productive days will happen when this is the only thing on your to-do list. Taking action comes with a sense of urgency. It's not something you do later; you do it now. Instead of drowning in the planning and ideation stage, start building, selling, or creating.

Best-selling author Robert Ringer stressed the importance of taking action In his book *Action! Nothing Happens Until Something Moves*. He said:

> *"An idea, of and by itself, has no intrinsic value. It must be accompanied by action. It is action that cuts the umbilical cord and brings an idea out of the womb. I can assure you that Fred Smith, the founder of Federal Express, wasn't the only person to come up with the idea of starting an overnight delivery service to compete with the woefully incompetent U.S. Postal Service...In fact, I would be surprised if literally thousands of other entrepreneurs weren't simultaneously mulling over the same idea. What made Fred Smith different from the rest of us was that he didn't just think about the idea; he took action. Action*

converts an idea into an experience. Action creates reality."[36]

BIAS TOWARDS ACTION

The easiest way to embrace the Key of Action is to be biased toward taking action. This means you should prioritize taking action on your ideas instead of overthinking or planning them. When you embody this bias, you're more likely to take steps to make things happen instead of getting stuck in the planning phase or waiting for the perfect opportunity. You need to be willing to take risks and make decisions quickly, even if you don't have all the info or need more confidence in your choice.

When you spend too much time planning, train yourself to feel a sense of unease. It should be an overwhelming feeling that you're wasting time. Stop what you're doing and switch gears. Do something that moves the needle. By "move the needle," I mean doing something that has a noticeable, measurable impact on your vision. This phrase is often used in creative endeavors to refer to making progress toward your goal. For example, an entrepreneur might motivate and encourage their team to take action by saying, "We need to move the needle on sales," to indicate that they need to only do tasks that increase sales significantly.

Being biased toward taking actions that move the needle is crucial to creativity. While thinking and planning are important, action will make real progress toward your vision. When you develop a bias towards action, you increase your chances of success. So if you have an idea you believe in, move the needle today.

---

[36] Ringer, Robert J. 2004. Action! : Nothing Happens until Something Moves. New York: M. Evans And Co.

Key of Focus

"One way to boost our willpower and focus is to manage our distractions and not let them manage us."—Daniel Goleman

THE UPSIDE OF CUBICLES

Have you ever wondered why the typical layout of office buildings is rows and rows of identical cubicles, each person confined to their own tiny space? These cubicles create an oppressive atmosphere where creativity comes to die, and it's designed this way intentionally. The objective is to keep people focused on their mundane tasks. Employees have time constraints, tight schedules, deadlines, and productivity goals. There's no time to chat with your co-worker or get distracted by the antics of those around you. Distractions in the workplace cost the company time and money.

On the other hand, employees use conference rooms and open-plan spaces to collaborate and brainstorm. These workspaces are where creativity thrives. That's why the eerie feeling of working in a lifeless office is most creator's biggest nightmare. Even though life-less spaces kill creativity, something surprisingly useful about them can enhance our creativity: the ability to focus intensely.

When we embark on our creative quests, our minds flow with ideas. I use the word "flow" because there are no gaps in the process. We are in a state of continuous, connected thought happening from moment to moment. Creativity flows when we are fully immersed in our work, present in each moment, and mindful of what we create. Even a tiny distraction can break this flow and cause us to lose focus. You can enhance your creativity and produce your best work by learning to focus intensely.

CHOOSE DISTRACTIONS WISELY

Like most things in life, distractions can be both good and bad. While they can disrupt our focus and productivity, they can also stimulate creativity. A Harvard paper titled "Unexpected Distractions: Stimulation or Disruption to Creativity?"[37] discusses the effects of unexpected distractions on creativity, citing that distractions can induce creativity in some settings. The paper explains how the creative process involves two cognitive sub-processes, divergent and convergent thinking. Divergent thinking happens when you generate new ideas. Convergent thinking occurs when it's time to decide which ideas to use.

During the idea generation phase, distractions can trigger new ways of thinking about your problems. Divergent thinking can benefit from these distractions. However, as cognitive overload brews, divergent thinking can diminish, and the creative flow can become blocked.

On the other hand, convergent thinking requires peak focus. During this cognitive phase, every distraction is disruptive.

By understanding how distractions affect these two types of thinking, you can learn to manage your focus and balance productivity and

---

[37] Wiruchnipawan, Wannawiruch. 2015. "Unexpected Distractions: Stimulation or Disruption to Creativity." Dash.harvard.edu, May. https://dash.harvard.edu/handle /1/17467526.

creativity. You will make the most of your creative sessions when you find the right balance of mental freedom and immersion.

HOW TO NOT SUCK AT WRITING YOUR FIRST BOOK

Before I started writing this book, I decided to skim through a few books on being an author. One of the books was *How To Not SUCK At Writing Your First Book* by Chandler Bolt. I'm embarrassed to admit that my insecurity about writing my first book attracted me to that title. While skimming this book, there was a gem that helped me on my writing journey that I'd love to share with you:

> *"Sometimes when you start writing you become overwhelmed by all the thoughts going through your head. As you write down one idea, another one will pop into your head that has nothing to do with what you are talking about...*
>
> *When that seemingly random idea appears, run with it. Don't put it on the back-burner out of fear it will steer you off course. Finish the thought that popped into your head and place it in the section of your book that it fits with the best.*
>
> *Then I want you to get back on track and start writing what needs to be written. You have to go with the feeling you get when you write."*

This excerpt is a perfect example of using distractions to your advantage early in your creative process. As I progressed throughout my writing journey, I eliminated more and more distractions. By the time I was working on the final draft, I was writing alone at 3 AM in the dark, with my phone notifications silenced.

DEVELOP A FOCUS RITUAL

Distractions are everywhere. They are a constant threat to our focus and productivity. You have to prepare yourself to eliminate them and get into a state of deep focus. That's why creative sessions like photoshoots and film sets have rules in place to maximize focus. Outsiders are not allowed on stage and phones are turned off. Craft an environment where you aren't at the mercy of what disrupts you. The optimal space should enable you to scale from complete mental freedom (i.e., loud music, multiple browser tabs open, other people, etc.) to complete immersion (i.e., silence, one primary app open, isolation, etc.).

Many of the greatest minds of human history had specific routines that helped them focus. Athletes performing at the highest levels have pre-game rituals that get them into the zone. Some authors have morning routines that allow them to hammer out thousands of words before noon. Some songwriters have nightly routines that give them the mental freedom to let their words flow on top of a beat.

Discover and craft a ritual that gets you focused every time you do it. Start by listing all the things that distract you during your creative process. Next to each of those distractions, write an opposing action you can take to eliminate it. Take all the solutions to your triggers and merge them into a routine that you do before you start your projects that require focus. For example, you might light a candle, silence your phone, put on headphones, or do deep breathing before you begin creating. Remember, the key is to find what works best for you and to be consistent. With practice, your focus ritual will become second nature, and you'll be able to enter a state of deep focus at will.

CAPTURING LIFE'S ENERGIES

We're always transforming. Whether we like it or not, each passing moment pushes us towards an uncertain future. This means that progress is always with us. It's an inevitable part of existing. Most creators progress by blowing in the wind, and I love that. Most times, that's the story of my life. There's a beauty in allowing the universe to transform you, willingly riding its ebbs and flows. But this path falls short if you desire to write your own story and choose how you grow. You're like a sailor navigating the sea of life. When the universe's wind takes hold of you, instead of freely blowing with it, you can adjust yourself to catch the wind and propel in any direction. Similar to the open sea, life is vast and unpredictable. The only way to get to where you want to go is by finding your lighthouse, a goal you can focus on. List areas of your life you want to blow in the wind vs the things you want to control. Go beyond your craft and artistry and think about your physical health, mental health, experiences, finances, relationships, education, spirituality, career, etc. Life will throw positive and negative energy along your journey; challenges, curve-balls, opportunities, luck. Capture this energy to propel you toward the person you desire to become. Remember, progress is inevitable. Change is inevitable. Evolving is inevitable. You will transform into anything you focus on, so leverage "focus" to create the life you want. So ask yourself, "Who do I want to become?". Now, religiously focus on that.

Key of Inspiration

"Inspiration is like ice cream. If you don't eat it now or store it for later, it will melt away in the palm of your hand."—Dwayne Walker

WHERE INSPIRATION COMES FROM

If you believe that generating ideas is the first phase of the creative process, you're wrong. Ideas are only as strong as their sources of inspiration.

Inspiration doesn't spontaneously come from within. After researching the world's best chefs, artists, writers, and inventors, it's clear to me that inspiration is all around us. All the time. When you're reading a blog about a fascinating concept, walking down the street observing other people, or even talking to a fellow creator, a dance of inspiration is happening—one beautiful idea after another. Our minds are consistently soaking in our surroundings and churning out inspiration. But most inspiration gets lost in the limitations of our memory.

Many creative people pull from their memory, experiences, and the people they admire. They wait until they are ready to generate an idea to start searching for inspiration. That's a flawed process. Creative geniuses do it differently. They don't wait for inspiration to strike or rely on a foggy memory. Instead, they make gathering inspiration a lifestyle.

When they read a passage in a book that makes them say, "Wow!", see someone wearing a shirt that they like, or hear something odd in a podcast, they instinctively do one thing: save it for later. They tune their mind to pick up on things they find remotely intriguing and document them in a place they can return to later. That's because they know how inspiration works. Even though it's not an inspiration they can act on immediately, it can still inspire them later.

THE RAP GOD

Marshall Bruce Mathers III, known professionally as Eminem, is one of the greatest hip-hop artists of all time. His contribution to the genre and accomplishments make him worthy of the title, but most importantly, it's the mastery of his craft. He's a true lyrical genius.

He bends the meaning and pronunciation of words to follow multiple rhyme schemes happening all at once. Repetition, alliteration, and metaphors are only a few tools he uses to tell captivating stories. His flow, speed, and tempo vary based on the beat. His mastery commands respect from some of the best lyricists in the industry.

The secret behind the depth and complexity of his lyrics hides in his writing process. While most rappers hear a beat and jump straight into songwriting, Eminem approaches it differently. He doesn't wait until a beat falls into his lap to write a song. Instead, Eminem collects inspiration for lyrics throughout the day. In an interview, he said, "I might find like six to twelve ideas and write them down. Just jot them down, and then at the end of the week or the end of two weeks, or whatever, I stack my ideas up and then I'm ready to write a rhyme."

That's the power of saving inspiration for later. Eminem knows that inspiration is fickle and fleeting. It abandons us as quickly as it comes. In a short writing session, most rappers may have three or four mind-blowing lyrics. Eminem, on the other hand, writes down genius lyrics all day. He doesn't worry about how it fits into a greater vision of a song. Most of his lyrical ideas never see the light of day. He only focuses on saving all his inspiration for later at whatever cost. He once said, "You really gotta live it. My mind 24/7, aside from family stuff obviously, is constantly thinking of ways to bend words. If I don't have paper, I'll write it on my hand or whatever. Sometimes when I fill up my hand then I'll transfer it to paper."

RESPECT TO THE FLEETING NATURE OF INSPIRATION

Here's and excerpt from an interview with Bob Dylan talking about the moment of inspiration behind his hit songs saying:

Bob Dylan: "*I don't know how I got to write those songs.*"
Interviewer: "*What do you mean you don't know how?*"
Bob Dylan: "*Those early songs were almost magically writ-ten...*

Darkness at the break of noon
Shadows even the silver spoon
The handmade blade, the child's balloon
Eclipses both the sun and moon
To understand you know too soon
There is no sense in trying

...Well, try to sit down and write something like that. There's a magic to that, and it's not Siegfried and Roy kind of magic. It's a different kind of penetrating magic. And I did it at one time."

> *Interviewer:* "*You don't think you can do it today?*"
> *Bob Dylan:* *shakes his head no*
> *Interviewer:* "*Does that disappoint you?*"
> *Bob Dylan:* "*Well, you can't do something forever. I did it once, and I can do other things now. But I can't do that.*"

THE MOMENT

A few months into dating my wife, Ife, we were in a mutually weary phase of deciding if risking our friendship to pursue a relationship was the right choice for us. One night, I was lying in bed listening to music. The moonlight burst through the window as I stared at the ceiling. Randomly, *Taiwa* by Marc Cary started playing. The piano chords instantly pulled me into a trance. Ife crossed my mind. I started thinking about all the feelings I've wanted to express to her but struggled to put into words.

I thought about how her aura burst into a gentle, calming shade of green. I thought about how closed off she was, like a shy turtle, but that I'm willing to be patient in the process of getting to know her slowly over time. Immediately, I started writing my thoughts down. "Green, gentle, turtle, Queen. Take your time coming out of your shell. I can't wait to see your skin…" I continued writing, empathizing with her past hurt, highlighting her natural beauty, celebrating our emotional and intellectual connection, and reassuring my desire to grow deeper with her. My hand wrote words faster than my mind conjured them. I lost all sense for time. When I finally paused, I stepped back and realized I created a poem that captured a pivotal moment: the moment I knew I fell in love with her. I still get goosebumps reimagining that experience and the purity in inspiration's magic.

SUPERNATURAL

Inspiration is an abstract yet tangible feeling. It's both pleasurable and rewarding. When it strikes, it's hard to know its source. And the result of leaning into your inspiration is creation.

Inspiration's elusive nature has led many people to believe it's divine. Divine inspiration is any supernatural influence upon humans that causes a person to experience a creative desire. Judaism and Christianity believe that people wrote the Bible out of inspiration from God. Hinduism has used music as a medium of achieving divine inspiration. Documents show ancient Greek muses as supernatural forces that gave artists their skill. Today, it's common for artists, scientists, and other creators to attribute their best ideas and creative impulses to supernatural or unknown forces. These are all examples of our collective effort to describe one shared human experience: Inspiration.

In researchers Todd Thrash and Andrew Elliot's paper *Inspiration as a Psychological Construct*, they tackle the experience of inspiration in what might be the most poetic research paper I've ever read.[38] They show that inspiration can be activated, captured, and manipulated. To acknowledge its abstract nature, they started the paper with a beautiful metaphor about breathing:

> *"In its literal sense, inspiration refers to the process of breathing in or inhaling, but it is the figurative sense that is relevant to psychology. The first figurative, general definition listed in the Oxford English Dictionary is the following: 'A breathing in or*

---

[38] Thrash, Todd , and Andrew Elliot. 2003. "(PDF) Inspiration as a Psychological Construct." ResearchGate. May 2003. https://www.researchgate.net/publication/1 0796715_Inspiration_as_a_Psychological_Construct.

infusion of some idea, purpose, etc. into the mind; the suggestion, awakening, or creation of some feeling or impulse, especially of an exalted kind.'"

Inspiration is a mental inhalation of your surrounding beauty. It fills your mind with ideas like oxygen to the lungs. The deeper you breathe it in, the more you feel alive. The more you focus on its breath, the more you feel in tune with yourself. It's always happening whether you choose to acknowledge it or not. While you're awake or while you're asleep. It's always coming. Always fleeting.

EVOKED, TRANSCENDENCE, AND MOTIVATION

Todd Thrash and Andrew Elliot conducted extensive research and studies and found three striking similarities between various accounts of inspiration.

The first is that inspiration is evoked. It feels more like something that happens to you than something you choose to experience. It's spontaneous and intrusive.

The second is that "inspiration involves transcendence of the ordinary preoccupations or limitations of human agency." This observation means that inspiration is noticeable because it doesn't feel like an everyday occurrence. It brings a moment of clarity, certainty, and awareness of new possibilities.

The third is "inspiration implies motivation, which is to say that it involves the energization and direction of behavior." An inspired person is moved by what triggers them. They're moved to produce, mirror, or transfer that inspiration into a creation.

Leverage these three keys to harness the power of inspiration. Train yourself to become familiar with the feeling. Not just the overwhelming feelings of inspiration but also the tiny sparks. Respect inspiration for what it truly is—a breath. You can't hold this breath forever. You have to let it go. In the moment of heightened motivation to act, creative geniuses always release it in a place where they can access it later. That is how you harness the power of inspiration.

* * *

Did this key spark an interesting thought?
Share it with me at WorldOfCreatives.com

Key of Dreams

"Through dreaming, we can perceive other worlds, which we can certainly describe, but we can't describe what makes us perceive them."—Carlos Castenada

A MELODY IN A DREAM

"I really reckon *Yesterday* is probably my best song." This statement is from Paul McCartney, the singer, songwriter, and musician who became famous with The Beatles. His song *Yesterday* solidified him as one of the most successful creators of all time. It holds the record as the most recorded song in history, with over 1600 versions. In 1980, Paul explained why *Yesterday* was his favorite song. "I like it not only because it was a big success, but because it was one of the most instinctive songs I've ever written."

Paul wrote *Yesterday* at 57 Wimpole Street, London. He slept in a cramped attic with only enough room to fit a bed and a piano. He slept there. He created there. These limitations of his creative space embodied the passion and hustle of a brewing creative genius. One night Paul had a dream. In that dream a melody spoke to him. He jumped up out of his sleep and started outpouring what will be later known as the first rendition of *Yesterday*.

Paul recalled that morning vividly:

"I woke up with a lovely tune in my head. I thought, 'That's great, I wonder what that is?'. There was an upright piano next to me, to the right of the bed by the window. I got out of bed, sat at the piano, found G, found F sharp minor 7th, and that leads you through then to B to E minor, and finally back to E. It all leads forward logically. I liked the melody a lot, but because I'd dreamed it I couldn't believe I'd written it. I thought, 'No, I've never written like this before.' But I had the tune, which was the most magic thing. And you have to ask yourself, 'Where did it come from?' But you don't ask yourself too much or it might go away. There are certain times when you get the essence, it's all there. It's like an egg being laid, not a crack or flaw in it."[39]

CREATIVITY AND DREAMS

How did one of the greatest songs of all time magically appear to its composer in a dream? Well, this is not a rare phenomenon for songwriters. Actually, many songs we love and enjoy are based on dreams. When an interviewer asked Eminem how his mind comes up with such complicated rhymes he said, "Oh, I wake up in the morning and they just fall out." ASAP Rocky also has a similar account as Paul McCartney. When ASAP described how creativity flows through him he said, "I dream and I wake up thinking about designs. I go to sleep sometimes and I think about rhymes, and I wake up and I have to remember it and put it in my phone and then go back to sleep. Sometimes you wake up in the morning and it's trash. Sometimes it's great." The benefit of documenting your dreams doesn't stop at

---

[39] "'Yesterday' by the Beatles. The In-Depth Story behind the Songs of the Beatles. Recording History. Songwriting History. Song Structure and Style." 2015. Beatlesebooks.com. 2015. http://www.beatlesebooks.com/yesterday.

songwriting.

James Cameron, one of history's greatest storytellers and filmmakers, is well known for his original stories *The Terminator* and *Avatar*. *Avatar* was a film based on the fantastical world of Pandora, possibly the most realistic depiction of an alien world ever depicted on the big screen. This film transports the audience light years across the galaxy. Every detail was meticulously thought out. The environment and bioluminescent plant life were based on the planetary location in its solar system. Every creature's biology evolved to fit perfectly, including the local tribe of Na'vi, a humanoid species indigenous to Pandora. *Avatar* was ahead of its time. James' vision was so realistic that he had to wait ten years after writing the script before filming the movie because the technology needed to make the film hadn't been invented yet.

Avatar was a success. It raked in over three-billion dollars in the box office. For every successful film, there's always someone else who claims they had the idea first. *Avatar* had ten lawsuit claims about the origin of this epic concept. James Cameron won all ten lawsuits with one key piece of evidence—a drawing.

James explained that he first thought of the idea for *Avatar* in a dream he had as a 19-year-old college student. In a feature for GQ magazine, James said:

> *"I woke up after dreaming of this kind of bioluminescent forest with these trees that look kind of like fiber-optic lamps and this river that was glowing bioluminescent particles and kind of purple moss on the ground that lit up when you walked on it. And these kinds of lizards that didn't look like much until they took off. And then they turned into these rotating fans, kind of like living Frisbees, and they come down and land on something. It was all in the dream. I woke up super excited and I actually drew it. So I*

actually have a drawing. It saved us from about 10 lawsuits. Any successful film, there's always some freak with tinfoil under their wig that thinks you've beamed the idea out of their head. And it turned out there were ten or eleven of them. And so I pointed at this drawing I did when I was nineteen, when I was going to Fullerton Junior College, and said, 'See this? See these glowing trees? See this glowing lizard that spins around, that's orange? See the purple moss?' And everybody went away."[40]

The idea for *Avatar* started from a dream and was developed over years to become the film we love today. James Cameron knew the power of harnessing his dreams for inspiration from a young age. Actually, *Avatar* wasn't the only story he created based on a dream. *The Terminator*, one of the most classic sci-fi action films of all time, also came to James in a nightmare. He was sick with a fever alone in a foreign city when his dream projected him into two characters from the future who were "out of sync, out of time, out of place."[41]

A few of the greatest scientific discoveries were inspired by dreams.[42] When Einstein was a child, he had a vivid dream of sledding down a hill approaching the speed of light. This dream was an inspiration for what was to become the Theory of Relativity. The father of quantum mechanics, Niels Bohr, developed the Bohr model

---

[40] "James Cameron Reveals 'Avatar' Franchise Came to Him in a Dream." 2022. Collider. November 24, 2022. https://collider.com/avatar-origin-story-james-cameron-drea m-comments/.

[41] Phillips, Ian. n.d. "James Cameron Came up with the Idea for 'Terminator' during a Fever Dream." Business Insider. https://www.businessinsider.com/james-cameron-came-up-terminator-during-dream-2015-6.

[42] Scientist, The Spaced-Out. 2015. "Dreams and Visions in Scientific Innovation." The Spaced-out Scientist. April 22, 2015. https://spacedoutscientist.com/2015/04/22/the-role-of-dreams-and-visions-in-scientific-innovation/.

of the atom after having an inspirational dream of electrons orbiting the nucleus like planets orbiting the sun. In 1869, Dmitri Mendeleev published the periodic table of chemical elements, which is arranged based on the elements' atomic and chemical properties. He said, "I saw in a dream a table where all the elements fell into place as required. Awakening, I immediately wrote it down on a piece of paper, only in one place did a correction seem necessary." His unconscious mind synthesized and organized the data that his conscious mind had been absorbing while working.

Dreams were the key to some of humanity's greatest contributions. These legendary examples of creative genius occurring in dreams feel magical, but it also feels oddly relatable. Have you ever spent a day struggling with an issue, but when you woke up the next morning you knew exactly how to solve the problem? Have you ever had a dream with a movie-like plot filled with great character development and an unexpected twist? These experiences are extremely common in creative people. The more scientists learn about the human brain, sleep, and dreaming, the more things seem to point back to creativity.

SLEEP EXPLAINED

Understanding the intricacies of sleep has always fascinated me. Sleep is a mysterious, uncharted land. It feels both familiar and foreign. Dreams can range from mundane to surreal, and yet the brain remains elusive in revealing the true workings of this mysterious state. Fortunately, through using modern brain-imaging devices, scientists are starting to uncover insights on the sleeping mind's relationship to creativity.

We know that the process of sleeping is much more complex than closing our eyes for the night. There are two primary types of sleep that alternate throughout the night: non-rapid eye movement (NREM) and rapid eye movement (REM). NREM sleep starts with a light doze and gradually becomes more profound, with muscles relaxing, heart rate and respiration slowing, and body temperature dropping. REM sleep typically kicks off around 90 minutes after the first NREM cycle and is the true deep sleep. Heart rate and respiration increase, and brain activity, as measured by EEGs, also increases, which is related to dreaming. This is why muscles are paralyzed during REM sleep, so you don't act out the dreams that are playing in your head.

SLEEP SCIENCE

According to cognitive neuroscientist Jessica Payne from Notre Dame University, dreams during the early NREM phase tend to be quite realistic, while the REM phase is when the brain's "binding errors" occur. This means that during waking hours, the brain is organized, but during sleep it is fragmented. This fragmentation can lead to unexpected connections being made. That's the beauty of sleep. It provides the chance to experience alternative and unexplored mental paths.

Research has shown that the REM state can have a positive impact on creativity. In one study, participants were tasked with solving a word puzzle I shared with you in the Key of Association called the remote-association test (RAT). In this challenge, the volunteers were presented with three words and needed to identify a fourth word that connected them. For example, the answer to "Fish", "Mine" and "Rush" is "Gold" because of the common connection creating "Goldfish", "Gold Mine", and "Gold Rush." After the first round of the test, the participants were asked to take a 40-minute nap. Those who experienced REM sleep during the nap demonstrated a 40% improvement in their scores on the follow-up test, while those who rested without REM showed a decline in performance.[43]

Another study at the University of Lübeck in Germany found that sleep can also sharpen our ability to find connections and solve problems. Participants were given math problems, but only 25% of the people found the answer. Surprisingly, when the volunteers were given the opportunity to obtain eight hours of sleep and then return to the problem, that percentage jumped to 59%. These studies show that sleeping on a problem opens your mind, allowing better solutions to reveal themself to you.

DREAM CAPTURING

The Key of Dreams explores the mysterious connection between our dreams and creativity. How many dreams of great ideas do you think you dreamt that's forever lost in your memory? You don't know. Thankfully, through scientific research and the experiences of these successful creators, we can identify key habits that help us unleash our dreams' creative potential. When I mapped out how creative geniuses were inspired by a dream, they all had one commonality: The creator documented the dream as soon as they woke up.

James Cameron drew pictures of the creatures in *Avatar* while they were fresh in his mind. Paul McCartney went straight to the piano to get the melody for Yesterday out of his head. When Dmitri dreamt of the periodic table, he "immediately wrote it down on a piece of paper." Creators do this because when a creative idea reveals itself in a dream, their window of opportunity to capture it is narrow. Scientists estimate that we forget 95% of our dreams within five minutes of waking up, so it's important to capture these fleeting moments of

---

[43] Kluger, Jeffrey. 2017. "How to Wake up to Your Creativity." Time. April 30, 2017. https://time.com/4737596/sleep-brain-creativity/.

inspiration.

To combat this ticking biological time limit of remembering dreams, keep a journal by your bed. Build the habit of writing and illustrating your dreams within five minutes of waking up. Sometimes you may wake up, start writing, and forget the dream halfway through. Don't get discouraged. Keep going. The more you build a habit of documenting your dreams, the more you will train your brain to recall your dreams without having to write them down. A recent study used brain imaging techniques to compare the brain activity of 55 people. In the group, 28 were high dream recallers and 27 were low dream recallers. The researchers found that high dream recallers scored higher on a measure of creative ability and had increased functional connectivity within a brain network known for dreaming and creative thinking.[44] This study reveals that as your dream recall muscle gets stronger, your creativity will strengthen too. Unravel the mysterious power behind our dreams. Unlock the ideas and inspiration speaking to you from your subconscious. Listen closely.

---

[44] Kluger, Jeffrey. 2017. "How to Wake up to Your Creativity." Time. April 30, 2017. https://time.com/4737596/sleep-brain-creativity/.

Key of Nature

"Look deep into nature, and then you will understand everything better."—Albert Einstein

THE BULLET TRAIN

In 1989, Japan's bullet trains reached speeds of 170 mph. Its speed was impressive, but it came at the expense of a few issues. It was so fast that it was causing noise pollution and structural damage. Japan tasked a team of engineers with making it quieter and more efficient.

Eiji Nakatsu, the development's general manager, shared an idea with his team that left everyone scratching their heads. His engineering or design background didn't inspire his vision for the future of the bullet train. Instead it came from his hobby of bird watching.

There's a remarkable bird found in nature called the Kingfisher. They're known for their large, sword-shaped beaks, which evolved to be perfect for hunting fish. They'd sit on a branch above water, waiting for the right moment to strike. When the opportunity presents itself, they dive at high-speeds, beak first, into the water, spearing their prey with their beak. They're in and out of the water in the blink of an eye. Their speed and efficiency are all credited to nature's design of its beak.

Eiji Nakatsu's vision for the bullet train was inspired by different components of birds, including the shape of the owl's wings and the sleek body of penguins. His most notable source of inspiration was the Kingfisher. He tasked the engineers to redesign the front of the bullet train to resemble the Kingfisher's beak. This one design implementation increased the train's speed and electricity efficiency and drastically decreased the noise and damage they caused.[45]

BIOMIMICRY

Throughout history, creative geniuses believed in the power of connecting with nature to enhance their creativity. Why? It's because nature is the most raw form of art. It's the baseline of all inspiration. If you reverse engineer the ideas and inspiration leading up to our top innovations, you will typically land on something in nature. This phenomenon comes from biomimicry, a design philosophy that looks to nature to solve our challenges. Biomimicry is a blend of science and art. By observing and studying the universe's natural problem-solving patterns, we take that inspiration and adapt our designs to create optimal solutions.

That's the creative power of biomimicry. It's not a new concept. For centuries, creators looked to nature for inspiration. Lu Ban invented the first Chinese umbrellas over 1700 years ago. His children inspired him when he saw them using lotus leaves to shield themselves from the rain. Ancient architects incorporated nature into structures for functionality and aesthetic. NASA studied gecko feet to develop more innovative adhesives. Scientists analyze bacteria chains interacting

---

[45] Vox. 2017. "The World Is Poorly Designed. But Copying Nature Helps." YouTube Video. YouTube. https://www.youtube.com/watch?v=iMtXqTmfta0.

with magnetic fields to improve GPS navigation devices.[46] Brands choose colors based on how they naturally make us feel. They use green, like the forest, to represent refreshment, peace, rest, and security. They use red, like fire, to represent excitement, passion, danger, energy, and action.

Nature's influence is vast. It's the most basic form of creativity. Lift the veil of everything we have created or everything we will create in the future, and you will find nature's influence. Everything starts there. We build on top of its elements because nature's most beautiful quality is its balance between being simple and elaborate. Everything in nature is highly complex but only as complex as it needs to be. Lao Tzu poetically described it, saying, "Nature does not hurry, yet everything is accomplished."

ATTENTION RESTORATION THEORY

When creators engulf themselves in nature, it unlocks something in them. For a long time, creators didn't know what mysterious energy they were experiencing. That was until psychologists Rachel and Stephen Kaplan developed the Attention Restoration Theory after researching nature's impact on human creativity.

Attention Restoration Theory suggests that while you spend time in nature, your concentration improves, and your brain operates at a heightened stimuli level for a longer time. This effortless brain function allows creative ideas to flow freely.

A study published by the University of Utah and the University of Kansas supported this theory. Participants who went on four to six-

---

46 "Y Studios — INSIGHTS | Passion | Y Studios — Biomimicry Design: Mother Nature's Influence on Products and Design." n.d. Y Studios. https://ystudios.com/insights-passion/biomimicry-design.

day wilderness hiking trips in nature showed a 50% increase in their performance on a creativity test compared to those who did not take the journey.[47] When you disconnect from technology and spend time in nature, you'll experience measurable benefits for creative problem-solving.

FINDING THE RIGHT "SPOT"

As that study revealed, any amount of nature is better than none. But while researching Attention Restoration Theory, Kaplan discovered that there are ways to increase the impact nature has on your creativity by choosing the correct location. Kaplan found that these four key factors[48] unleash this theory's optimal effects:

1. Extent: You have to feel immersed in the environment. Every sensual stimulus around you should be from nature. Embrace the sound of the ocean waves crashing, the palm trees blowing in the breeze behind you, and the ocean's vastness as far as the eyes can see. Every element plays an important role.

2. Being away: You must be so far away from your responsibilities and everyday habits that you can't even do them if you want to. Don't allow your brain to lose focus by your typical day-to-day distractions.

3. Soft fascination: If you find things in your environment exciting and novel, it will be easier to stay mentally present. Intriguing

---

47 University of Utah. 2012. "Nature Nurtures Creativity after Four Days of Hiking." ScienceDaily. December 12, 2012. https://www.sciencedaily.com/releases/2012/1 2/121212204826.htm.

48 Ackerman, Courtney. 2019. "What Is Kaplan's Attention Restoration Theory (ART)? Benefits + Criticisms." PositivePsychology.com. July 10, 2019. https://positivepsych ology.com/attention-restoration-theory/.

environments will inspire you in ways you can't predict.

4. Compatibility: You have to feel comfortable in the environment. If you feel anxious the entire time, your mind won't have the freedom to expand. Find a space in nature where you feel comfortable exposing your true self. Surrender to that environment.

MOTHER NATURE

The inspirational pull of Mother Nature is undeniable. Her overwhelming beauty and universal balance have been a driving force for great thinkers, poets, writers, and painters. In *The Starry Night*, Van Gogh painted the magic of the wind and stars. Beethoven was known for taking long walks in nature to find inspiration for his musical compositions. J.R.R. Tolkien, the author of *The Lord of the Rings*, drew inspiration from the natural world to create detailed fantasy environments.

Tap into nature's rich source of inspiration. You can use it straightforwardly to optimize something you are building or more abstractly, like writing a poem using the ocean to represent the vastness of the human experience. Find an immersive and comfortable spot in nature. Go there when you face creative challenges and look to nature for inspiration and guidance. Open your mind to the clarity that emerges from the energy it gives you.

Key of Patterns

GARY V

In 1978, a family of nine fled the communist regime in Belarus by migrating to the US. They settled in a cramped studio apartment in New Jersey. The father worked hard at a liquor store, eventually purchasing it. His journey sparked an entrepreneurial spirit in his son, Gary Vaynerchuk, who went on to become a renowned figure in the business world.

Gary V, as he is commonly known, developed his entrepreneurial instincts at a young age. He started by selling lemonade and baseball cards, making up to $3,000 a weekend when he was 14. As he put it, "when you have $30,000 in cash under your bed, and you're not selling weed, you're doing a good job."

Gary honed his salesmanship working at his dad's wine and liquor store. He kept an open mind and stayed curious about the products and the customers. He had a deep desire to understand what drove their purchasing decisions. Gary once said, "I think I'm a great salesman because I listen and watch. I'm behavioral. It's hunting. I look for patterns. I pay attention to what people do." One day he realized that his customers preferred shopping with someone who was a wine connoisseur. Around the same time, social media was taking off. Gary's instincts kicked in. He combined the trend of social media and his knowledge of wine. First, he renamed his dad's store to Wine Library and bought WineLibrary.com. Then he capitalized on the growth of the internet by being one of the first businesses to set up an e-commerce store. Lastly, Gary started WineLibraryTV, a long-form, episodic YouTube show where he sat down, tasted wines, and authoritatively talked about them. This strategy was a success, and Wine Library grew into a $60 million business.

PATTERN RECOGNITION

Gary's entrepreneurial journey didn't stop there. He invested in companies like Facebook, Twitter, Uber, and Venmo and opened a social media marketing company, VaynerMedia, which works with Fortune 500 brands. He was also an early adopter of e-commerce, social media content, and blockchain technology. Today, the world respects his ability to predict and combine future trends.

Gary Vaynerchuk's business success is largely due to his exceptional pattern recognition skills. While most people consume information, only some understand how to connect the dots. Gary instinctively connects seemingly unrelated dots. This skill enables him to plan, organize, and execute ideas in budding niches long before other people see its value.

Pattern recognition can help you approach creative challenges from new angles. It encourages blending genres of music or styles of art. It allows entrepreneurs in every industry to stay ahead of their competition. It helps fashion designers predict stylistic trends in society.

The best way to develop this skill is through pattern-recognition tools. Mind mapping is one of the most common tools. Let's explore the power of mind mapping and how you can use it to unlock your pattern recognition abilities.

THE SCIENCE BEHIND MIND MAPPING

Dr. Roger Sperry's Nobel Prize-winning research uncovered the brain's cortical skills and how they enable us to process inputs such as words, colors, and images. Cortical skills refer to various abilities associated with the cerebral cortex, such as perception, attention, memory, language, and problem-solving, which are important for cognitive functioning and learning. In the 1960s, Dr. Sperry conducted groundbreaking experiments on a patient with a severed corpus callosum, which bridges the brain's two halves. He discovered that the same stimuli given to each eye caused the patient to respond in oddly specific but different ways.[49] This observation led to the discovery that both halves of the brain practically function independently and are responsible for different cortical skills.

However, the most interesting outcome of his research was that the higher the number of cortical skills involved in absorbing a piece of information, the better you learn and process the information. It showed that the brain processes visual information better than verbal or textual information. Ralph Haber's work, published in *Scientific American*, affirmed this. His research showed that nine in ten people could recall more details of an image than a text block. That's why it's hard to remember someone's name but not their face.

These two revelations about how we process information and learning give mind mapping its potency. You convert your thoughts

---

[49] Lienhard, Dina. 2017. "Roger Sperry's Split Brain Experiments (1959–1968) | the Embryo Project Encyclopedia." Asu.edu. December 27, 2017. https://embryo.asu.e du/pages/roger-sperrys-split-brain-experiments-1959-1968.

(verbal information) into drawings (visual information). A mind map is a visual representation of how ideas connect. It is an effective tool for developing ideas or organizing your knowledge creatively.

ORGANIZING YOUR IDEAS

Knowing which mind-mapping technique to use will maximize your creative output. There are five mind maps you should integrate into your mental toolbox.

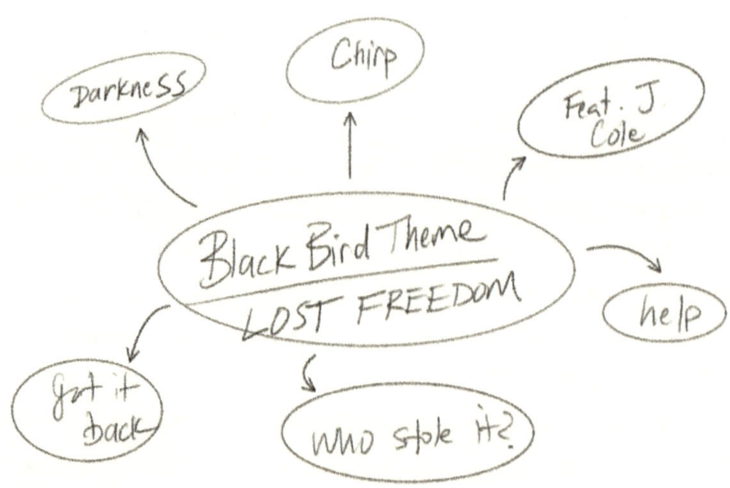

Radial

Radial mind maps are a good choice when you want to show the connections between a central idea and a large number of related ideas. These mind maps organize around the idea, with branches radiating outwards in all directions. This map is similar to the hierarchical map, except these are one-off ideas instead of subcategories. A musician might use this to brainstorm ideas for a new album, with the central idea being the overall sound or theme of the album and the branches representing different songs or ideas for songs.

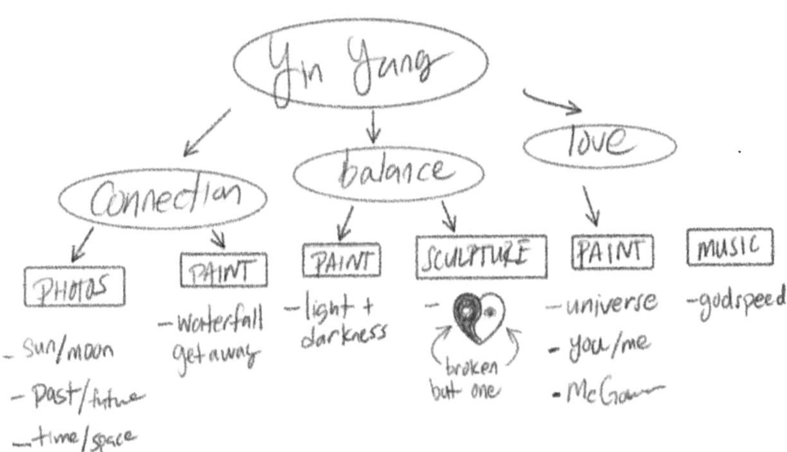

Hierarchical

Hierarchical mind maps organize information around a central idea, with branches representing sub-ideas or categories. Use this technique to plan out the structure of a creative project, with the main ideas at the top and sub-ideas arranged underneath. For example, an artist can plan out a series of paintings, with the main idea being the overall theme and the branches representing different paintings or ideas for paintings within that theme.

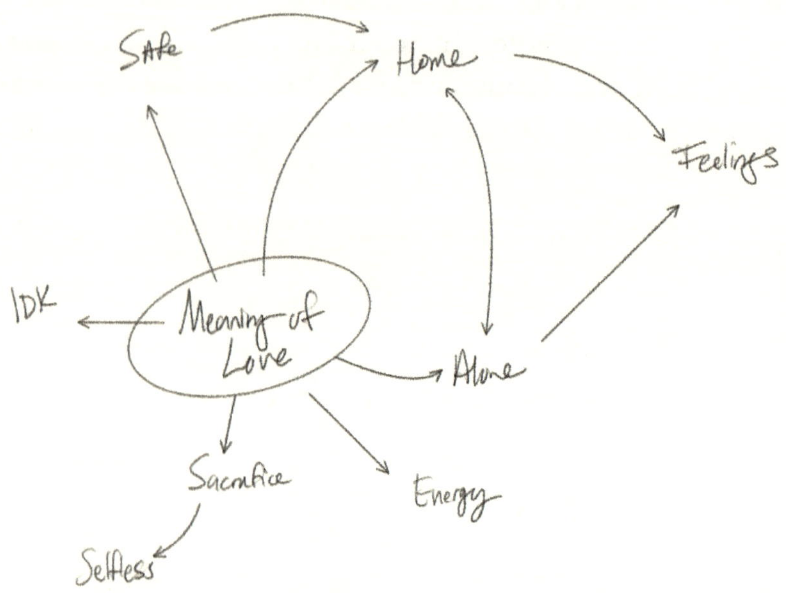

Concept

Concept maps are a good choice for illustrating the relationships between concepts or ideas. These mind maps focus more on showing relationships between concepts rather than individual ideas. For example, a researcher might use a concept map to explore the connections between different theories in a particular field, with the central idea being the overarching subject and the branches representing different theories and their relationships to one another.

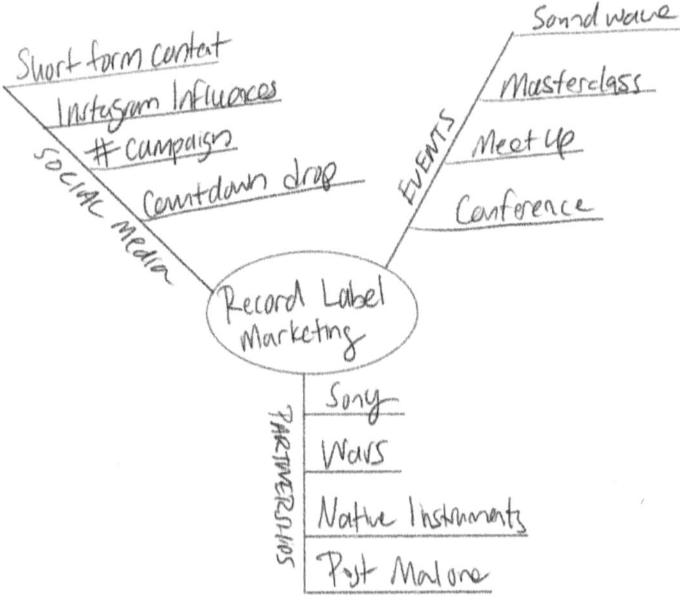

Spider Diagram

Spider diagrams are a good choice when you want to brainstorm different ideas for specific subcategories. For example, you might use a spider diagram to generate ideas for a new marketing campaign. The central idea could be the campaign theme, the branches representing different marketing channels, and marketing ideas stemming from those branches.

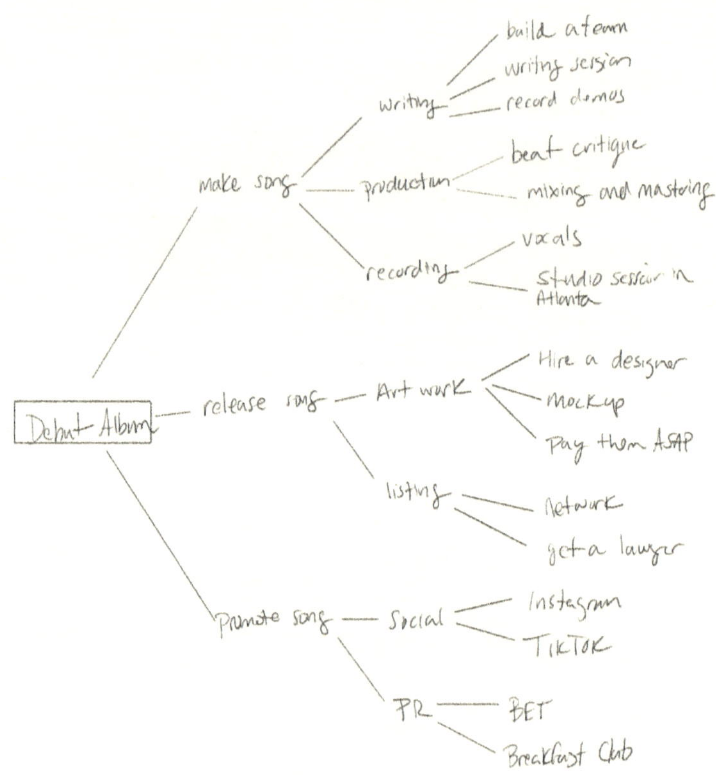

Tree Diagram

Tree diagrams are a good choice when you want to show an idea's evolution or a process's progression. These mind maps are more linear, with branches arranged in a tree-like structure. Tree diagrams help show how different ideas build on one another over time. For example, you might use a tree diagram to map out the steps in releasing a music album. The main branches represent the stages of the process, and the sub-branches represent the specific tasks or actions involved in each stage.

MAXIMIZING MIND MAPPING

When it comes to brainstorming, the mind map is an invaluable tool. When you get an idea, your mind sparks off a host of related thoughts until you have a web of interconnected ideas in your head. Mind maps essentially capture this process. When used correctly, they help you build on your creative ideas while ensuring you remember everything along the way. In a single glance, a mind map offers both a bird's eye view and a detailed look at the elements involved in a project or idea. Writers, for instance, use different types of mind maps to sketch a novel's plot, develop characters' personalities and backstories, or plan interactions between characters as the story moves forward.

Here's how a writer might approach developing a character's backstory for their novel. First, they may start by writing the character's name in the whiteboard's center with a circle around it. Then, they create branches that lead to other circles. Within each of these new circles, they can put different aspects of the character's personality. One could talk about his relationship with his parents, while another could talk about hobbies and quirks. These branches can then further branch out with backstories on how the character came to develop these facets of himself. As the writer builds similar mind maps for other characters in the story, it can organically reveal avenues for interactions between characters. Maybe two characters share a love for hiking which arose from their time spent with boy scouts. Perhaps they could have met there as children and become lifelong friends or enemies.

The beauty of a mind map is that it doesn't have to make sense to anyone else. It is a tool to streamline your thoughts and explain something to yourself. You can visually represent your ideas using colors, images, and symbols. Start small and simple, and build up to more complex maps. Draw arrows to show how different ideas connect and analyze the map to reveal new directions and possibilities. Use this powerful tool to develop your thoughts. Put your brain on paper. Make uncanny connections. Unravel the boundless potential of your mind.

Key of Emotion

"Rational thoughts never drive people's creativity the way emotions do."—Neil deGrasse Tyson

MULTI-BILLIONAIRE EMOTIONAL TYCOON

Saying Oprah Winfrey changed the broadcasting industry would be a gross understatement. Oprah stands in a creative league of her own. She created and humanized a new genre of TV, tabloid talk shows. Oprah's philanthropic efforts gave a voice to marginalized communities. She broke racial and financial barriers, becoming the first African American multi-billionaire. Her sociopolitical acumen, a deep awareness and appreciation of her emotions, and how she told emotive stories fueled her success.

For decades, she connected emotionally with the people she interviewed on *The Oprah Winfrey Show*. Oprah and her guests opened up and bravely shared their pain. She single-handedly created the confessional format that's commonly used in talk shows today.

At the cusp of her meteoric rise, *TIME* wrote, "Guests with sad stories to tell are apt to rouse a tear in Oprah's eye or get a comforting arm around the shoulder. They, in turn, often find themselves revealing things they would not imagine telling anyone, much less a national TV audience. It is a talk show as a group-therapy session."

Her empathetic stance shattered stereotypes and continually broke new ground. The Oprah Winfrey Show was simultaneously praised and criticized. For instance, when she interviewed Ellen Degeneres, Ellen came out as gay. Over 40 million people watched the episode. It sent ripples of both affirmation and indignation. When Oprah asked Ellen why it was important to come out as gay herself, she responded, "I realized that as long as I had this secret, that I worried about all the time, that it made it look like something was wrong." This episode paved the way for many other people to feel safe enough in themselves to come out. Over the years, they're both praised by the LGBTQ+ community, Ellen for her bravery and Oprah for guiding Ellen in using her emotions as a vehicle for truth.

RESONATING EMOTIONALLY

Stories, music, paintings, and other creations that pluck at our heartstrings are in our DNA. Whether good, bad, funny, sad, inspiring, or gut-wrenching, emotive art forms reach deep within our consciousness and stir up something ancient and powerful. This energy is why creatives who enhance their emotional awareness create things that resonate with a large audience.

When speaking to the *Grapevine*, Oprah said, "As a storyteller, I think the ability to create a narrative that people can relate to, feel a part of, and feel connected to is the dream of everybody who uses words to allow people to see and feel their own humanity." Emotional art lowers people's defenses and gives them permission and validation to feel their inner truth.

CRAFTING LOVE

Bowerbirds are considered artists in the animal kingdom. Male bowerbirds build complex sculptures that rival the craftiness of most humans. They intricately decorate it with colorful feathers, sticks, stones, berries, plastic, and glass. The choice and arrangement of these decorations are extremely intentional; different species have different preferences for design and medium. The bird spends weeks (about 10 months in human-years) gracefully creating their masterpiece. Once they're done, the sculpture serves as a stage for the male's courtship dance, a series of movements, poses, and sound effects, to attract his female counterpart.

I've always opted to express my deepest emotions through art. Especially love. While I was writing this book, I was also working on a top secret art show that has since become the pinnacle of my creative output thus far. Like a bowerbird dedicating his time to crafting a romantic body of art, I spent a year discreetly ducking off to my art studio working on ten large-scale paintings to present to my lover to ask her for her hand in marriage.

When she walked into the art show, each piece was covered in black sheets. The entire show was a journey back in time through our love story, back to the moment I knew she was the one for me. So we started along the journey unmasking each piece one by one. Each artwork embodied a significant moment in their relationship, a cherished memory, or a pivotal epiphany. Each piece was also paired with one of our favorite love songs, creating an immersive and sensual experience. At each step of the way we reminisced on our relationship, admired the art, and vibed out to the music. This multi-sensory exhibition not only allowed us to reflect on our past but also set the stage for a future together. In the end, when I popped the question, she didn't just say, "Yes," she said, "Yes, duh!". That's the power love has on creativity and the power creativity has on love. You can find a link to a video of our proposal in the footnotes.[50]

THE POWER OF LOVE

Most creative geniuses have a lovely muse. Some of the most outstanding art and literature were born from love. Pablo Picasso's love for French artist Françoise Gilot inspired some of his most famous works, including the *War and Peace* series. Dante Alighieri's unrequited love for Beatrice Portinari inspired his poetic masterpiece *The Divine Comedy*.

The sonnets of Shakespeare, Van Gogh's paintings, and Beethoven's music are all examples of love's power to inspire creativity. These works of art aren't just beautiful. They're incredibly human, conveying the depth and richness of our emotions in a way that only creativity can.

Love has a remarkable impact on our cognitive abilities. It makes us sharper and more creative thinkers. Take the case of Stephanie, a researcher at Dartmouth College, who designed the "Love Machine" test.

Stephanie invited women who were in love to try out her "Love Machine." The test involved flashing the participant's name of their romantic partner on a computer screen for a quick 26 milliseconds. This speed was only long enough for the participant's brain to register the name subconsciously. The test then measured the participant's ability to complete creative tasks following the subconscious imprint of the partner's name.

---

[50] YouTube. (2023). Art Show Marriage Proposal. Retrieved January 16, 2024, from https://www.youtube.com/watch?v=dJ-aNzsJvbY&t or visit www.worldofcreatives.com/into-fayne

Stephanie found that when she subconsciously primed participants with their beloved partner's name, they performed significantly better on the task than when she primed them with the name of a platonic friend. This effect was due to how love excites the neurons in our brains. Love releases dopamine and stimulates recently evolved brain areas associated with creativity, intuition, autobiographical memory, complex language, and imagination. Love plays a highly complex role and completely changes our way of thinking creatively.

At its core, love is all about connection. Love's bond brings us together with others, whether that's in romantic relationships, friendships, or family. It lets us see the world from someone else's perspective, feel their feelings, and create ties that last a lifetime.

Creativity, at its core, is all about expression. It's how we articulate our thoughts, feelings, and ideas authentically. Creativity allows us to explore the limits of our imagination, break down barriers, and build something entirely new.

Love and creativity are a match made in heaven. It's the blend of connection and expression. Allow yourself to love deeply and freely. Be willing to open yourself up to the world, new experiences, and the people who matter most. Push yourself beyond your comfort zones, and face the unknown depths of love with an open heart.

MOTIVATIONAL INTENSITY

There are clear benefits to making your craft as emotional as possible, but the link between emotions and creativity goes beyond anecdotal evidence. Dr. Eddie Harmon-Jones conducted research over seven years about emotions and motivational intensity. Motivational intensity is how strongly your audience would feel pulled toward or pushed away from something you create. The studies show that the most vital benefits don't come from the *type* of emotion you use in your art; it comes from the *intensity* of the emotion. High intensity draws people in regardless of whether it's a positive or negative emotion.[51]

As scary as it sounds, you have to choose to feel deeply as a creator. Don't bottle in how you feel. Express it through your craft. Creativity thrives in the unknown, where fear and uncertainty reign. It's where you'll find the courage to be real, vulnerable, and creative enough to make something unique and beautiful that will have a lasting impact on the world around us.

Often, creative people live fulfilling lives. The insights and perspectives they gain knock on their heart's door begging to be expressed. Ultimately, we don't only wish to experience the fullness of our emotions internally, but also to share them with our audience. Expressing yourself is the surest way to speak authentically in your craft.

So let's embrace how we feel. Let it fuel our creativity. Create with the purpose, passion, and conviction that your emotions conveyed through your art will endure long after we're gone.

---

[51] Kaufman, Scott Barry. 2015. "The Emotions That Make Us More Creative." Harvard Business Review. August 12, 2015. https://hbr.org/2015/08/the-emotions-that-ma ke-us-more-creative.

Key of Limitations

"We need to first be limited in order to become limitless."—Phil Hansen

THE SIX-WORD STORY

Ernest Miller Hemingway was one of the greatest American writers of the 20th century. He coined a style of writing that exercised the reader's intellect and wisdom. The style is known as the Iceberg Theory. The Iceberg Theory is a minimalistic style that allows readers to infer underlying deeper meanings by letting them shine through the words instead of explicitly stating them. He mastered the power of knowing what not to say. Hemingway wrote elegantly while conveying most of the information and emotion in a few words. He believed that the meaning of a story should be hinted at and left to the reader's interpretation, like an iceberg where only a small part is visible above the water while the majority is beneath the surface.

There's a tale about when Hemingway was challenged to limit his creative freedom. He was having lunch with fellow writers, and Hemingway claimed he could write a six-word story. The writers were reluctant to believe that anyone, regardless of their talent, could write a story interesting enough to capture the hearts of the reader in six words. Hemingway sensed the denial in their voice. He told them to each place a ten-dollar bet on his ability to accomplish this feat, and they instantly agreed.

Grazing his mustache softly, Hemingway thought deeply while his peers continued to enjoy their food. As lunch was wrapping up, the other writers nagged him with boastful comments about how they planned to spend the most effortless ten dollars they'd ever made. Suddenly, Hemingway's eyes lit up. He reached across the table, grabbed a napkin, and pulled a pen from his shirt pocket. He quickly jotted down six words on the napkin and passed it around the table. The table grew strikingly silent. Tears streamed down their faces.

The words read: "For sale: baby shoes, never worn."

FLASH FICTION

This general concept of telling a story with the absolute minimum of words is known today as flash fiction. Flash fiction is an ultra-short form of storytelling that emphasizes brevity and efficiency. Flash fiction has many types defined by word count, including the 50-word "minisaga," the 100-word "microfiction," the 750-word "sudden fiction," and the 1,000-word "flash fiction."

These stories convey an entire narrative arc using precise language and imagery. It often focuses on a single character, moment, or idea. Flash fiction shows us that creativity can fit within limitations while offering deep emotional triggers.

CHOICE PARALYSIS

When creators experience a creative block, it often stems from a psychological effect called choice paralysis. Choice paralysis happens when we're presented with too many similar choices. Not only are we less likely to choose effectively, but we also get less satisfaction from our selection.

The more choices we have, the more negative emotions and stress we have. These negative experiences can accrue to the point that they outweigh any joy we derive from making a choice. It can completely drain our energy, rendering us incapable of acting on our choice even after we have made it. Without constraints, creativity can lead to complacency. Psychologists refer to this phenomenon as the path of least resistance, where individuals settle for the first intuitive idea that comes to mind rather than pushing themselves to develop even better ideas.

NATURAL LIMITATIONS

Interestingly enough, what we perceive as creative freedom still has natural limitations. We are already limited creatively by the bounds of the universe. Only 94 naturally occurring scientific elements exist, such as carbon, hydrogen, and oxygen. Think deeply about that limitation, and you will realize that those 94 elements make the entire universe—every star, every planet, every animal, every human, every landscape, and everything humans ever built.

THE KEY INNOVATION

Innovation is creative geniuses' response to limitations. In one remarkable example, GE Healthcare's MAC 400 Electrocardiograph (ECG) transformed access to medical care in rural areas.[52] The secret to its success was a set of seemingly impossible constraints

---

[52] Acar, Oguz A., Murat Tarakci, and Daan van Knippenberg. 2019. "Why Constraints Are Good for Innovation." Harvard Business Review. November 22, 2019. https://hbr.org/2019/11/why-constraints-are-good-for-innovation.

that were placed on the engineers tasked with its development. These constraints included creating an ECG device with cutting-edge technology, costing no more than $1 per scan, being lightweight and portable enough to fit into a backpack, and relying solely on battery power.

With only 18 months to complete the project and a budget that was ten times smaller than that of its predecessor, the engineers had their work cut out for them. However, the goal, time, and resource constraints fueled their creativity and led to their breakthrough ECG innovation that ultimately succeeded.

LIMIT YOURSELF

You don't always need to think outside of the box. Constraints force you to be more selective and intentional in your creative process. For example, Dr. Seuss' editor challenged him to write a book using the constraints of a limited vocabulary. He wrote "Green Eggs and Ham" with only 50 different words and sold millions of copies.

By forcing yourself to work within defined parameters, you're challenged to think creatively and find solutions that might not have been possible otherwise. Experiment with giving yourself complete freedom and then apply various guidelines. Progressively make the boundary of your limitations smaller and smaller. Create your own rules and experiment with them. The goal is to create a puzzle piece that fits within those bounds.

Embrace limitations and strategically impose them on yourself. Give yourself a set amount of time to work on a project or develop an idea. Try creating something using only a specific type of medium or tool. Give yourself a theme or topic. Sometimes a unique answer is right in front of your face. By honing your attention on the elements in front of you, you'll force yourself to break things, put them back together, experiment, fail, learn, and, eventually, create.

* * *

Did any of these keys spark an interesting thought?
Share it with me at WorldOfCreatives.com

Key of Stories

YOU SHOULD BE A GRIOT

When comedian Dave Chappelle received the Mark Twain Prize for American Humor in late 2019, he joined a select group of African-American comedians to win comedy's highest honor. In a touching moment during his acceptance speech, he reminisced about his mother encouraging him to be a storyteller during his childhood:

> "We had a real oral tradition in our house. I knew the word 'griot' when I was a little boy. A griot was a person in Africa who was charged with keeping the stories of the village. Everyone would tell the griot their stories and they would remember them all so they could tell future generations. When they got old, they'd tell them to someone else. And they say in Africa, when a griot dies it's like a library was burned down. My mother used to tell me, before I ever thought about doing comedy, she said, 'You should be a griot.'"

In West African communities, the griot holds a revered position as a master storyteller. Their responsibility is to safeguard their people's cultural traditions and oral history. Their creativity is essential to the ongoing vitality and preservation of their culture. They pass down stories, songs, and proverbs from one generation to the next. Griots weave enchanting narratives using repetition, rhyme, and metaphor to captivate their audience. Their storytelling performances are a feast for the senses, often incorporating dance, humor, and other artistic expressions. Griots demonstrate the profound influence of stories on society.

As Dave Chappelle pointed out, storytelling is a creative act with a larger purpose. It's one of the most effective ways to transfer knowledge. Stories of all kinds allow us to experience the world more fully. It is an art form that enables us to remember our collective past and is the most effective way to validate and share our experiences and ideas.

PEOPLE LOVE TO RELATE

Talking to Tony Robbins, the comedian-turned-media-mogul Kevin Hart also talked about telling stories through the medium of comedy. At first, he thought stand-up comedy was strictly about being funny. However, over time, his perspective shifted as he observed his audiences' reactions. "People love to relate," he says. "People love to see what's real. You love to identify. If I sat up here and I talked about things you guys couldn't identify with, or couldn't walk away and go, 'Wow,' I'm alienating myself from my crowd. The best way to open up and make myself a part of my crowd is to be real. Because we all love *real*. My life, my mistakes, my ups, my downs, my marriage, my divorce, my kids, that's what we all share. We just share it differently. We all travel. If you don't travel, you want to travel. If you want to travel, where do you want to go? There are so many things that I can break down that act as connective tissue between me and everybody. I can relate to everybody in this room and I don't have to change who I am."

The power of storytelling is the key to conveying your message and connecting with your audience. The beauty of storytelling lies in its ability to engage someone's emotions, imagination, and memory in a way that facts and figures cannot. By sharing a compelling story, you can break down walls and connect people from various backgrounds, cultures, and experiences.

A well-crafted story can help us see the world through someone else's eyes. We get so emotionally invested in stories that they can shift our entire way of thinking. They can inspire life-changing epiphanies. They motivate us to take action. When we hear a tale of triumph over adversity, we are inspired to believe we can accomplish the same challenges. Stories can help you share a vision for the future and give your audience the courage to take the necessary steps to make it a reality.

ANATOMY OF A STORY

So what is the essence of a great story? Dan Harmon, the creator of the massively popular Adult Swim series *Rick and Morty*, breaks the anatomy of storytelling down into eight essential parts:

1. You: A relatable character who pulls the audience in, in circumstances where they feel comfortable.
2. Need: The main desire that initiates the story.
3. Go: How the character enters a new set of circumstances beyond their comfort zone.
4. Search: How the character deals with the discomfort of the new situation.

5. Find: How the character finds what they desire.
6. Take: The price (often heavy) the character pays to get what they want.
7. Return: How the character returns to their original circumstances.
8. Change: How the journey changes the character and what lessons they pick up along the way.

Good storytelling mirrors life. In fact, you may even look at this template and realize that this is how we store memories in our minds. The best stories, therefore, are not necessarily about outward journeys, although the external factors of a story are crucial. They are, in essence, inner journeys.

Great stories make us feel as if we were walking in the character's shoes. We feel their hope and despair, share their fears and ambitions, and ultimately either root for them or wish them harm. In any case, great stories make us emotionally invested in the lives of their characters.

TENSION AND RELEASE

Creators commonly misunderstand storytelling as a tool only used in writing. It obviously works well in songwriting or a novel, but it is challenging to understand when discussing dance, music, and art. Creative geniuses know how to integrate the power of storytelling regardless of their craft. They do this by applying two abstract elements found in great storytelling: tension and release. Tension builds suspense and conflict within the story, while release provides resolution and closure.

Consider the case of storytelling in jazz. Traditionally, jazz music has been an interplay between a rhythm section and a lead section.

The rhythm section sets a familiar stage, establishes internal musical coherence, introduces familiar melodic motifs, and sets the tempo and grooves in which the piece will unfold. The rhythm section's job is to create a familiar tonal landscape where the listener can settle and feel at home before the lead section takes center stage.

The lead section is where the magic happens. The lead section features soloists who *talk to*, or *talk at*, this tonal landscape. Sometimes they politely agree with it. Other times they may boldly dissent and veer off into uncharted territory, allowing their improvisational instincts to take over. That's when the music gets exciting and unpredictable.

This sense of musical conflict that builds up to the feeling of either a positive or a negative outcome, is what makes a great story, no matter what your medium. It's the tug of war between the rhythm and the lead section. It's the tension and release.

All forms of creativity can use tension and release to keep an audience engaged. It creates a sense of anticipation and emotional investment. In music, you can feel tension through dissonance, repetition, or unexpected changes in tempo or rhythm. Chords containing dissonances are considered "unstable." When we move from the dissonant chord to a stable chord, we feel a weight lifted off our shoulders. This release is what musicians call resolution.

Painters create tension in their art with the use of contrasting colors or textures. They then release that tension through symmetry and balance. Dancers use deliberate movements, sudden pauses, and asymmetrical poses to create tension followed by fluid movements synchronized with music to release it. Even chefs use tension with bold flavors and exotic ingredients and release it in the balance of presentation and textures.

Identify the tension and release hidden under the veil of your creative projects. Leverage it to keep your audience engaged and invested in the story behind your work. Make them look inward. Make them the story's main character where they feel the weight of the tension and release in the message you're trying to convey.

Key of Sharing

"We don't do this kind of work for awards or to be recognized. We do this to share stories with the world."—Daniel Berehulak

TUPAC SHAKUR

Ask anyone in the hip-hop scene about the greatest rapper of all time, and you are bound to hear the name, Tupac Shakur. They will usually respond with reverence for his craftsmanship and sadness over his untimely demise. For many people, Tupac was the first person to give a voice to their lives by telling their stories. His brutally honest yet engagingly imaginative style brought the struggles of the African American community to the forefront of American discourse.

His expressiveness became the hallmark of his life and intensified as he grew up. In his interview with *E!*, he described how he uses music to respond to unfair treatment, such as being beaten by the police. "In my rhymes, it vents that anger because I can fire back at the police and I won't go to jail for life. My music, and a lot of this music, it's only talking about the oppressed rising up against the oppressor," he remarked.

Telling stories and spreading positive ideas was something that not only came naturally to Tupac but was something he considered essential. The ideas in Tupac's lyrics tackled complex issues that were often ignored by mainstream media and politicians, such as social injustice, poverty, and racism. But Tupac's impact went far beyond politics. Through his music, he challenged the traditional views of masculinity. He spoke openly about his emotions and vulnerabilities, breaking down barriers and encouraging emotional expression among young men. The ideas in his music ignited important conversations and debates, sparking a movement of social consciousness among his listeners. Tupac's iconic music and ideas continue to resonate with society.

THE EVOLUTION OF IDEAS

Your role as a creator is to create and inspire. That's why you need to create and share your ideas with people. Once an idea is out of your mind, its success is in the hands of the people it inspires.

Your ideas can't live on past you if you don't share them. Ideas want to be released so they can fight to survive in the mind of our shared human consciousness. The survival of ideas works like the theory of natural selection. You see, Darwin's theory doesn't strictly apply to living organisms; it also applies to abstract entities, like ideas.

Similar to organisms in the physical world, ideas are subject to the battle for existence. Their right to exist depends on their ability to resist extinction by rival ideas. These ideas can be music trends, fashion statements, marketing slogans, languages, scientific theories, art styles, or any other creation.

THE GLADIATOR

I had thirty-seven ideas for the title of this book. I thought of *How to Be a Creative Genius, The Starving Artist,* and *Creative AF,* just to name a few. Instead of relying on gut instinct to pick one, I let my ideas compete like evolution. I decided that the best way to select an idea was to release them into the world and let each fight to the death. I created a few mockup designs of the book, each with a different title. I took all of those photos and paid for Facebook ads for each of them. About 30,000 people saw the ads, and thousands of people who were interested in buying this book clicked the ads. After weeks of testing, the book titles with the most clicks were *Create or Die*, *48 Laws of Creativity*, and *Born to Create*. But in the end, only the strongest survived. And the victor? Well, that's the title gracing the cover of this book.

YOUR IDEAS NEED CRITICISM

John Gould, the editor that Stephen King apprenticed under, shared a key piece of advice about writing that bleeds into creativity as a whole. He said, "Write with the door closed, rewrite with the door open." When you create an idea, it starts off being solely for you. The journey starts off lonesome. Once you deem the work as complete, the idea belongs to anyone who wants to love it or criticize it.

Here's what Walter Lippmann, a Pulitzer Prize-winning journalist, shared about the value of having opposing forces that fight to either nurture or kill ideas:

> *"The conservative who resists change is as valuable as the radical who proposes it—perhaps as much more valuable as roots are more vital than grafts. It is good that new ideas should be heard for the sake of the few that can be used; but it is also good that new ideas should be compelled to go through the mill of objection, opposition, and contumely; this is the trial heat which innovations must survive before being allowed to enter the human race. It is good that the old should resist the young, and that the young*

should prod the old; out of this tension, as out of the strife of the sexes and the classes, comes a creative tensile strength, a stimulated development, a secret and basic unity and movement of the whole."

According to Walter Lippmann, conservatives and radicals each have valuable societal roles. While traditional ideologies provide stability like the roots of a tree, we should still consider new ideas. This tension lets only the most innovative ideas survive.

ANTI-AUTOGRAPH

I rarely sign my artwork. It's a bad habit, I know. I've received backlash for it my entire creative life. Historical evidence suggests that signing art dates back to ancient civilizations. It's an unspoken rule with unknown origins. I know I should sign my art (and I swear I want to), but I often just simply forget to. Growing up, my parents, art teachers, and friends tried to drill in my head that signing my art was a requirement, but something about signing art feels unnatural to me. It always has. I think it stems from an opinion I have about art.

To me, creating art feels like the most raw form of creation: having a child. Do you feel like your parents own you or do you feel like an individual? A lot of parents feel like just because they created you they have ownership over you. I understand their sense of responsibility for your wellbeing or sense of appreciation and awe at creating life, but I battle with the idea of ownership. They created you, but they don't own you.

In that same view, I don't own my art. Yes, I arranged raw materials in a way that's provocative, but that's it. I feel that same sense of parental responsibility over my art. I want it to be great. I want it to be preserved. I want it to inspire and influence. But I don't want to own it. I want to simply appreciate it in awe. I want people to value it based on how it makes them feel, not because I'm the artist that brought it into this world. I'm not advocating for everyone to stop signing their art, but I believe the perspective that's best for my art, and maybe art in general, is to share it with the world and give it the space and freedom to take on a life of its own.

GET OUT OF YOUR WAY

Sharing your ideas through your creative work without worrying about the fear of judgment is vital to your creative health. You're the only person who can accurately share your unique perspective. There are billions of people on this planet. No matter how niche you may think your creative practice is, the truth is that millions of other people will resonate with your ideas. It will speak their truth to them in a better and braver way than they ever could on their own. Don't be afraid to take up space in this gigantic world. There's more than enough room for your creative voice.

Of course, everything doesn't have to be shared. Random thoughts you scribble in your poetry journals, raw rehearsals with your band, or unfinished paintings can remain private. But when it comes to your creative output, the answer to whether it's good enough to share is always a resounding "Yes." Many creative people hold themselves back with an unchecked desire for perfectionism. It limits their willingness to share their ideas. The truth is that every creator has aspirations that exceed their current skills, but growth and improvement come with experience and time. Waiting for an arbitrary "good enough" benchmark will only stifle, rather than enhance, your creativity. Remember, your ideas are needed, and there is enough room for them to flourish.

HUMAN'S GREATEST FEAR

One of the bravest things a human can do is share their art with the world. You see, while many people might be afraid of things like spiders or death, public speaking is the most common fear in the world. Imagine standing up in front of a crowd of ten thousand people and giving a speech. The feeling of your heart dropping in your chest and the butterflies rumbling around in your stomach is an instinctual human experience.

Sharing your art is an even bigger and more unknown fear. When you share your art with the world, it's like going up in front of that same crowd of ten thousand people and giving a speech about your deepest feelings, your struggles with depression, your controversial opinions, your traumatic experiences, and all of the raw and authentic parts of who you are as a human being. It's hyper-vulnerable, and it's the most authentic peek into the truth of a person.

I understand the fear dancers have about going on stage, artists have about posting their paintings on social media, and writers have about releasing their books. I really do. But when you take note of the lives of history's creative geniuses, it's best to stand up for your ideas, even when it's scary. If you don't, nobody else will. Your creations will only be spread as far as you allow them to. So, let them blossom. Take that leap of faith and share your work with the world. Because when you do, you never know who might be touched, inspired, or changed by what you've created.

Key of Apprenticeship

"A smart man makes a mistake, learns from it, and never makes that mistake again. But a wise man finds a smart man and learns from him how to avoid the mistake altogether."—Roy H. Williams

KING OF HORRORS

Stephen King, the celebrated author of horror, thriller, drama, and science fiction, has undoubtedly left a mark on the literary world of the 20th century. He rightfully earned the title "king of horrors" from the bone-chilling fear he evoked in his readers.

After nearly being suspended from his high school for writing a headline that teased his teacher, Stephen's guidance counselor tried to redirect his writing skills to something more constructive. They offered Stephen a sports reporter job position working under an editor named John Gould. He reluctantly accepted.

John Gould set a tone of mutual respect that allowed Stephen to open up a bit more. He was patient with Stephen. Stephen didn't know much about sports, and this was the first time anyone had offered to pay him for writing. The first piece Stephen wrote was about a local baseball game. When he turned it in, Gould took out a pen and went to work on it, circling and crossing out mistakes and suggesting edits.

This moment was the first time someone took Stephen's writing and showed him their thought process behind improving it. He pointed out the strengths and weaknesses of his work. In the end, the marked-up piece was a work of art. It was such a beautiful chaos that Stephen said it "deserves to be framed."

Stephen learned to value constructive criticism and used it to improve his writing. He credits these editing sessions with Gould as helping him develop his writing style and teaching him how to write more concisely. He learned that to be successful, he had to be willing to put in the time and effort to apply these criticisms to develop his craft. In Stephen King's book *On Writing*, he credited Gould with providing him the best writing education he's ever received, saying, "I took my fair share of English Lit classes in my two remaining years at Lisbon, and my fair share of composition, fiction, and poetry classes in college, but John Gould taught me more than any of them, and in no more than ten minutes."

THE BEST WAY TO LEARN

In the realm of creative subjects, the type of education you pursue can have varying impacts on your creativity.

Take learning from a book, for example. While books can offer valuable insights and time-tested tactics, they are often laden with fluff, leaving you to sift through a sea of information to find the relevant nuggets. While learning from your mistakes is certainly useful, avoiding unnecessary mistakes is even better. Learning from literature struggles to answer one crucial question: What time-tested tactics are still relevant today?

Then there's formal education, such as attending art, film, or culinary school. While this option can provide you with a solid foundation of techniques and industry standards, you risk falling behind as standards change. After all, by the time you've mastered the subject matter taught in school, the standards necessary to thrive in today's world could shift entirely. This cycle will leave you working intensely on your craft for years, just to lift your head one day wondering how the world has changed so fast. Formal education lacks answering another vital question: What new-found tactics are the most important to learn?

Learning on your own is another viable option, and one that I highly recommend. You can experiment and get a grasp on your inner abilities and their relationship with the craft. You will learn a lot about the current state of the world, but you'd lack the answer to one important question: Where is the world going?

Now, there is one form of education that combines the best of each learning style: apprenticing under a master. While securing such an opportunity can be challenging, it's well worth the effort.

Masters in their field don't waste time on fluff; instead, they focus on implementing time-tested tactics optimized for today's era. They possess a deep understanding of their craft's history and seamlessly apply it to their creations. The tactics they use today are the tactics that will be taught in tomorrow's textbooks.

QUALITIES OF A PERFECT MATCH

Choosing the wrong mentor can set you up for failure. If you trust someone to show you the ropes, but their knowledge is flawed, you will waste your time. It's better to learn alone than to learn the wrong things from someone. Spend time validating who you choose to mentor you. The best mentor depends on your personal goals, but here are the five core qualities to keep an eye out for:

1. Mastery: Find a mentor who is considered a master in their field. When someone effortlessly knows the intricacies of the craft,

they can guide you, too. If they haven't achieved anything you consider notable or you desire for yourself, keep on searching.

2. Creativity: Find a mentor who can teach you to think outside the box, explore new techniques, and develop your unique style. If they try to force their style onto you, they will hinder your personal growth.

3. Communication skills: Find a mentor who can teach you in a way that you understand. To teach complex concepts and provide feedback on your work, a mentor has to be excellent at conveying their thoughts to you. The best mentors can't hold themselves back from sharing knowledge. If you haven't learned anything from them before you pursue the apprenticeship, move on and find a mentor who loves teaching.

4. Passion: This is the most underrated quality of a mentor. A passionate mentor will inspire you to fall in love with your craft. They instill the integrity needed to appreciate the nuances and pursue your dreams with enthusiasm. If talking about their work doesn't make them smile, you will have a miserable apprenticeship.

5. Patience: An essential quality to look for in a mentor is their ability to give you the support and guidance you need to develop your skills without making you feel like a nuisance. Find someone willing to understand the level you're at and meet you where you are.

The value in finding the perfect match to apprentice under is that you will learn faster and more practically. It will give you a glimpse into the future of your industry and how you can fit in or disrupt it. By working alongside a professional, you gain valuable experience in a real-world setting.

MIRROR NEURONS

There are a group of neurons in the front of your brain that fire whenever you move or perform specific actions like stroking a paintbrush, performing a dance move, or playing a key on a piano. In the 90s, a group of neuroscientists discovered something shocking. Their study revealed that 20% of those neurons were activated not only when humans do something but also when humans see someone else doing that same action.[53] This study is fascinating because it means your brain mentally simulates other people's actions. When you observe other people, it's treating their actions as if you're doing them yourself so that you can mimic them. These clusters of neurons are called mirror neurons.

Mirror neurons are only found in humans and primates, bringing an amusing deeper meaning to the saying "monkey see, monkey do." Mirror neurons allow us to transfer knowledge exceptionally quickly compared to other animals. By doing what we see, ideas can be passed to people around us and generations to come. In his TED Talk, Vilayanur Ramachandran, a neuroscientist, explained how this aspect of mirror neurons swiftly advanced humans[54] saying:

"This [adaptation of mirror neurons] made evolution suddenly Lamarckian instead of Darwinian. Darwinian evolution is slow. It takes hundreds of thousands of years. A polar bear to evolve a coat will take thousands of generations, maybe a hundred

---

[53] Ramachandran, Vilayanur. n.d. "The Neurons That Shaped Civilization." Www.ted.com. https://www.ted.com/talks/vilayanur_ramachandran_the_neu rons_that_shaped_civilization.

[54] Ramachandran, Vilayanur. n.d. "The Neurons That Shaped Civilization." Www.ted.com. https://www.ted.com/talks/vilayanur_ramachandran_the_neu rons_that_shaped_civilization.

thousand years. A human being, a child, can just watch its parent kill another polar bear and skin it and put its fur on its body and learn it in one step. What the polar bear took a hundred thousand years to learn, it can learn in five minutes, maybe ten minutes. And then once it's learned, it spreads by geometric proportion across a population."

These mirror neurons are how humans naturally transfer knowledge of tools, shelter, language, and more. They're responsible for yawning when we see a friend yawn, crying when they're sad, and laughing when they laugh.

LEARN BY MIRRORING

Our brains' ability to imitate others' actions is a powerful learning tool. Apprenticeships leverage this cognitive tool. Since we learn by mimicking, there's no better way to master your craft quickly than by getting up close and personal to imitate a master.

Approach your apprenticeship as if you had the opportunity to resurrect a legendary creative genius from the past. Observe their techniques, styles, and creative process in real time. Imitate them. By mirroring their behavior, you can learn from their successes and incorporate some of their strategies into your work.

If they're open to it, collaborate with them on a project. You will get a closer peek into their thought process behind every tactic. This side-by-side execution and comparison will elevate your craft. At the end of it all, you will have a project that showcases your growth.

Seek constructive feedback from them. Don't let your emotions toward your creative work hold you back from growth. Think of the bigger picture. A high-quality constructive criticism of your work now can have a positive effect on your craft indefinitely. When you receive feedback, consider how you can incorporate it into your future creations.

Lastly, but most importantly, use mirroring to develop your unique style. Learn the foundations, but apply them in ways that are authentic to you. Don't force their style on you. Don't aim for perfection. Aim for understanding and application. Your goal is not to become your master—it's to find a master within yourself.

Key of Flow

"The best moments in our lives are not the passive, receptive, relaxing times. The best moments usually occur if a person's body or mind is stretched to its limits in a voluntary effort to accomplish something difficult and worthwhile."—Mihaly Csikszentmihalyi

KOBE BRYANT

Kobe Bryant, one of the greatest basketball players of all time, was known for his legendary ability to perform under pressure and make clutch plays in crucial moments. On April 14, 2004, during the Los Angeles Lakers game against the Portland Trail Blazers, Kobe added another unforgettable moment to his legacy.

This game was pivotal for the Lakers, as they needed to win to secure the second playoff seed in the Western Conference. The match was intense, with both teams trading leads throughout the night. The self-proclaimed "Kobe Stopper," Ruben Patterson, was defending Kobe.

With the Lakers down by three points and time running out in the fourth quarter, they turned to Kobe to keep them alive. With his back against the wall, Kobe caught the ball behind the three-point line, dribbled, and pump-faked, but Ruben Patterson stayed put and used his body to build a wall between Kobe and the basket. With tactical precision, Kobe leaned to his right and jumped around Ruben's body to put up the long-distance shot. Swish! The shot sunk into the basket, and the crowd went wild. The commentator said, "Kobe Bryant ties the ball game up in a way only Kobe Bryant can do."

As the game headed into overtime, Kobe remained in the zone, knowing the battle wasn't over yet. The score continued going back and forth, sending the game into double overtime, a rare occurrence for basketball games. Now, the Lakers needed to hit two buzzer-beaters in one game, a near impossible feat. The odds weren't in their favor.

With only one second left on the clock and the Lakers down 102 to 104, they needed to score another miraculous three-pointer to win the game. Kobe took charge, running to the perimeter, catching the ball with his back to the rim, spinning swiftly to find a defender's outstretched arm in his face, and releasing a shot that was arched high enough to go over their hand. As the ball soared through the air, you could hear a needle drop in the arena. And then, swish. The shot found the bottom of the net, securing the victory for the Lakers and sending the stadium into a frenzy of celebration.

This moment has since become one of the most iconic buzzer-beaters of all time, cementing Kobe's reputation as one of the most clutch players in the history of the NBA. His ability to perform under pressure and consistently execute made him a beloved and revered player.

HOW DID HE DO IT?

Kobe's fearless approach, especially in the last seconds of a game when the pressure was at an all-time high, earned him the nickname "The Black Mamba." His ability to knock down shots when it mattered the most was one of his many legendary traits. When he was in that zone, it was famously known as the Mamba Mentality. Kobe's supreme confidence, his ability to stay present and in the rhythm of the game, and his unwavering focus were all key elements of his mindset.

From the outside looking in, you can see when Kobe taps into the Mamba Mentality. It's in his eyes and unwavering emotions. It seems like his body is here, but his mind is elsewhere. People always wondered what happened in his head when he tapped into that mindset. One day Kobe described what exactly happened in those moments, and it wasn't what anybody thought. He said:

"When you get in that zone, it's just a supreme confidence that you know it's going in. It's not a matter of if or this-that. It's going in. Things just slow down. You know, everything slows down. You're here. You just have supreme confidence. But when that happens, you really do not try to focus on what's going on because you can lose it in a second. Everything becomes one noise. You don't hear this or that; everything's just one noise. You're not paying attention to one or the other. We just stay right there. Really try to stay in the present and not let anything break that rhythm."

In those moments, time moved slower. The noise from thousands of people cheering disintegrated into nothingness. His body moved effortlessly, seemingly making shots on command. His coordination heightened. What type of mystical trance was he experiencing?

THE FLOW STATE

What Kobe described is called the flow state. It's a universal experience that creators go through. It's a highly focused state of consciousness that feels superficial. It puts you in a trance. Like Kobe, other athletes, artists, scientists, and creators from all industries describe the flow experience using similar words. They experience time moving slowly, fast, or sometimes even non-existent. Hunger, thirst, and the need for sleep become irrelevant. Their movements become automatic as they effortlessly execute at their highest potential.

The first person to research the flow state was the psychologist Mihaly Csikszentmihalyi. He interviewed hundreds of creative professionals across a broad spectrum of the arts and identified critical ingredients that can spark the flow state.

First and foremost, the difficulty of the creative task must be well-matched to your skill level. If the challenge is too easy, you'll quickly become bored. If it's too difficult, you'll become frustrated and overwhelmed. You have to find balance. When you're engaged in something that's both challenging and within your abilities, you're much more likely to enter a state of flow.

Secondly, the task must be absorbing, demanding your complete attention and involvement. This undivided attention is a far cry from mindlessly scrolling through social media or watching TV. Instead, it would be best if you were fully immersed in the activity, using your mind and body to its fullest potential. This immersion makes time feel like it's bending.

Thirdly, the creative task must have clear objectives or parameters, so you can see progress and success as you work. Goals like "becoming a great artist" are too broad and vague to be useful here. Instead, specific targets that are measurable and achievable, such as "painting a portrait in under an hour," are more likely to lead to a flow state.

Finally, and perhaps most important, the motivation to engage in the activity must come from within. External rewards like money or fame are nice, but they're not enough to sustain a flow state. To truly experience flow, you need to be internally driven, fueled by your own sense of purpose and passion. When all these elements come together, you'll find yourself in the elusive state of flow where time stands still, peak performance becomes effortless, and you're completely immersed in the present moment.

GROUP FLOW STATE

Group flow state, or collective flow, is another incredible phenomenon that occurs when a group of individuals experiences a shared state of flow, allowing them to work seamlessly together as if they are part of one entity. While it's often recognized in team sports like basketball, soccer, or football, people in other settings such as musical bands, dance compositions, or business brainstorming sessions experience it, too.

In 2000, Phil Jackson became the head coach of the Lakers after winning six NBA championships with the Bulls. He made meditation and mindfulness a mandatory practice for the team. He'll turn the lights out, and the team trained their minds like they train their bodies. Kobe Bryant commented on how it impacted the team, saying, "Honestly, I bought into it. I bought into the meditation. I bought into the deeper connection that exists within the game. And so when you watch our teams, or you watch any of Phil's teams, we were never rattled ever because we're always in the moment. Always in the present. Always extremely calm. Always looking at the reality of the situation and not letting our emotions cloud our execution, and that comes from being in a meditative state that he would teach from day one."

If you want your team of creators to engage in group flow, there are three things you need to do. First and foremost, you need to work towards a common goal with a clear mind. While some fields may have an inherent set goal, if you need a defined shared goal, it's important to create one that's measurable, challenging, and achievable.

The second key factor is ensuring each person has a clear role within the group. Similar to sports, where different people play positions requiring completely different strengths and weaknesses, everyone in your team needs to know their role and how to play it effectively to achieve group flow.

Lastly, your team needs to trust each other. Each position on the team needs to feel comfortable leaning into their strengths while allowing their teammates to compensate for their weaknesses. If your group checks all three of these boxes, magic can happen.

HYPOFRONTALITY

According to cognitive neuroscientist Arne Dietrich, the flow state can decrease activity in our prefrontal cortex, the part of our brain responsible for memory and consciousness. This temporary down-regulation, known as transient hypofrontality, is also a symptom of neurological medical conditions like ADHD, bipolar disorder, and schizophrenia.

But don't be alarmed. In the flow state, this hypofrontality allows the subconscious mind to take the wheel, facilitating communication between different areas of the brain that don't usually interact. Hypofrontality causes the experience of distortions in time, loss of self-consciousness, and silencing of our inner critic. It sounds like a psychedelic drug.

The flow state is a powerful state of mind that allows individuals to operate at a higher level of consciousness. Creative geniuses know how to achieve flow at will. Just watch Steve Jobs delivering an epic speech, Serena Williams dominating a tennis match, or Beyoncé's flawless performances on stage—they all operate in the flow state, where their subconscious mind takes over, and they perform their best.

Tapping into the flow state can be a game-changer for creators and performers alike. By achieving a state of intense focus, you can elevate your performance and achieve feats that might otherwise be impossible. By setting the right conditions for flow to occur, you can achieve peak performance in whatever you do. With practice, you will be able to experience flow at the snap of your fingers.

* * *

Did any of these keys spark an interesting thought?
Share it with me at WorldOfCreatives.com

Key of Meaning

"The aim of art is to represent not the outward appearance of things, but their inward significance."—Aristotle

DRAKE

Drake is renowned for crafting some of the most successful and influential hip-hop and pop music. His music strikes an emotional chord with his fans. In an interview, he said, "I create music at a different pace than everybody else, and I think I would attribute that to the fact that in order to get in there and really make something, it has to have some emotional value." One of his key strategies for achieving this is infusing his lyrics with themes of personal growth, relationships, and challenges. He strictly writes from his personal encounters and struggles but communicates them in a way that speaks to the universal experiences of his listeners.

Drake creates his relationship with his fans through his art. He doesn't speak much about his personal life to the public outside of his lyrics. For his audience to understand who he is, he methodically creates meaning in his work.

When rumors leaked that Drake had a baby, social media attacked him for hiding that he had a kid. Drake didn't take interviews or post on his social channels. Instead, he released a song called *Emotionless* and rapped one line that silenced all criticism: "I wasn't hiding my kid from the world, I was hiding the world from my kid, from empty souls who just wake up and look to debate. Until you're staring at your seed, you can never relate." Drake's lyrics allowed people to understand the deeper intentions behind his actions. It showed that his actions were a deliberate form of fatherly protection.

While many mainstream artists prioritize making their songs catchy, Drake prioritizes encapsulating relatable moments and meanings. For instance, in his hit single *Marvin's Room*, Drake sings about using alcohol to cope with his breakup. He captures the impulse to reach out to an ex-partner, resonating with anyone who has ever struggled through a painful heartbreak. Similarly, in *God's Plan*, Drake tackled the subject of gratitude and the significance of giving back. In the music video, he donated $1 million to various people, charities, and organizations in need. The lyrics resonate with listeners who desire to utilize their blessings to help others.

Drake's exceptional talent weaves profound meaning into music and pulls in a broad and diverse audience. It's the foundation of his career. By tapping into universal themes and experiences, he creates a sense of empathy and understanding that connects with his listeners at a personal level.

CREATING WITH A DEEPER MEANING

Seth Godin, the Godfather of Marketing, said, "People don't believe what you tell them. They rarely believe what you show them. They often believe what their friends tell them. They always believe what they tell themselves." It's a simple truth. If a marketer can get a person to tell themselves a story about a product, with themself as the main character, the person will buy and share that product with their friends.

Creativity works the same way. The deeper you make your message, the more it speaks to your audience's core being. Your music can calm someone before they walk out on stage to make a speech, or your painting can offer comfort to someone dealing with loss. These deeper connections allow your creations to etch stories into the minds of others.

Your audience will see themselves in your art, right at the center of the story. When you achieve this level of relatability, your audience becomes your greatest advocates. They'll enthusiastically recommend your calming music to a friend that's nervous for their first performance or your comforting painting to pick up a friend when they're feeling down. Your art acts as a medium others can use to transfer emotions, advice, and ideas they may struggle to express themselves.

SYMBOLISM

Throughout human history, we used symbols to transfer knowledge and deeper ideas in an easily understood and memorable way. Ancient Egyptians painted hieroglyphic symbols on the walls to tell stories. Religions rely on symbolism to spread their beliefs and values. The Christian cross serves as a reminder of Jesus' death and resurrection. The Om is a symbol in Hinduism that represents the three states of consciousness and the fourth state beyond the physical world. Businesses like Nike and Apple use symbolism to build brand messaging and loyalty. Symbols are found everywhere in every culture for one reason: They work.

Symbolism communicates complex ideas and emotions in a simple, memorable way. That's why it's at the core of branding for countries, religions, businesses, and more. That's why it's called branding. It's no different than farmers branding their cattle, painfully searing a design in their skin. Branding in society is taking an idea and permanently stamping it into the minds of its target audience.

As a creator, you can to use symbolism in your work to have a deeper connection with your audience. Symbolism looks different based on the medium you're using. It's hidden behind the metaphors of a song, the objects in a painting, and the movements in a dance. Use symbolism to embed layers of meaning into your creations. Having multiple layers of meaning opens up your creations to be interpreted in different ways, allowing the viewer to discover new unpredictable insights and connections.

REMAIN AUTHENTIC

Billie Eilish is a young and influential artist who has made her mark in the music industry with her unique sound and open approach to expression. Her ability to connect with fans through her music, along with her willingness to address important issues, has solidified her status as a living legend in contemporary music. A key to her success is her ability to remain authentic to who she is regardless of rise in fame.

Eilish is known for being open about her struggles with mental health, body image issues, and the challenges she faced as a young artist. She doesn't shy away from discussing her vulnerabilities and insecurities in an industry that often prioritizes polished images. This level of honesty resonates with fans on a personal level. Eilish's voice makes her fans feel seen and less alone in their own struggle. As a result, Eilish's fans religiously trust her music because she doesn't present a facade or project an image that contradicts who she truly is. Her authenticity breaks the barrier between celebrity and fan, fostering what feels more like a unique friendship.

Every day, a new product is trending, a song tops the charts, or a hilarious meme goes viral. It can be tempting to box yourself into the deeper themes behind what's popular. The problem is that thinking this way will push you further from your true self. Your authenticity will decline.

Creating with authenticity means creating based on situations, values, and emotions you've experienced yourself. If you stray from this, your audience will see right through you. Your art will touch on topics without penetrating the surface. Varying levels of authenticity are why some love songs make you cry while others make you cringe. The only way to improve your creative authenticity is to gain a deeper understanding of your life, values, and beliefs and then try to grow the courage to express what you uncover about yourself. It's an intimidating process, but always remember that millions of people have experienced what you experienced and are struggling to express themselves. They are out there searching for exactly what you are capable of creating. They want to feel understood through your art. A creator's courage is another person's solitude.

Ultimately, when it comes to creating meaningful work, it's all about connecting with your audience on a deeper level. And to do that, you need to authentically weave profound themes and symbolism into your work. By tapping into your own universal experiences and values, you will create a sense of empathy that allows your audience to feel one with your work. Edgar Degas, a famous French Impressionist, once said, "Art is not what you see, but what you make others see." Your work has the potential to inspire, uplift, and transform lives. Gain an understanding of who you are. Then help others see you.

Key of Learning

"Anyone who stops learning is old, whether at twenty or eighty. Anyone who keeps learning stays young."—Henry Ford

CHARLES BUKOWSKI

Charles Bukowski is one of the most controversial yet intriguing American writers and poets. He had a reputation for writing raw, unfiltered, and unapologetically honest pieces about the darker aspects of life. The vices depicted in his work spanned from drinking and gambling to graphic violence and sex. His work was a reflection of personal demons he struggled with throughout much of his life. Even though his writing rubbed many people the wrong way, his body of work expressed a sense of compassion for people who struggled with similar life experiences.

Before he received success as a writer, Charles clocked in thousands of hours perfecting his craft by writing every day for nearly twenty-five years. He maintained a rigorous writing schedule throughout his life, often waking up early to write before heading off to his day job. During that time, Charles read and studied the work of Dostoevsky, Hemingway, and Celine. He experimented with their techniques and styles and applied them to his writing.

After decades of learning the craft, Charles Bukowski published his debut novel, "Post Office," at fifty years old. At an age when most people would start planning their retirement, Charles' mind was fully alive, absorbing life by engaging with it deeply. Over the rest of his career, he published five more novels and dozens of poems.

BEGINNER'S MIND

There's a Zen Buddhist principle called beginner's mind. First popularized in the West by Shunryu Suzuki, the beginner's mind, or Shoshin, is a nuanced way of looking at the world. Shunryu described this concept by saying, "The mind of the beginner is empty, free of the habits of the expert, ready to accept, to doubt, and open to all the possibilities." This way of thinking creates the mental conditions necessary for constant learning.

Shoshin requires that we drop all expectations and preconceived notions that we may have about any aspect of our craft. This mindset enables you to approach the world with a sense of openness, curiosity, and a willingness to learn.

Think about the last time you learned something about your craft you were proud of. Sure, there was some confusion, but the novelty of what you were trying to learn was also exhilarating. This feeling of awe that comes from learning is only achievable when you tap into the Shoshin mindset. Our best research on learning shows us that we drift away from learning things that don't bring us joy. Joyful learning can lead you to a better relationship with your craft and yourself rather than getting bogged down with limiting beliefs and self-defeating thoughts.

FALLING IN LOVE WITH THE CRAFT

Bukowski's lifelong commitment to continuous learning, practice, and experimentation demonstrates the importance of remaining a student of your craft. He was enthusiastically devoted to understanding the intricacies that made a story engaging and a sentence flow. Charles Bukowski fell in love with the art of writing.

Leonardo da Vinci once said, "For, verily, great love springs from great knowledge of the beloved object, and if you little know it, you will be able to love it only a little or not at all." Great love comes from a great understanding of the thing you love. The more you delve deeper into a topic, a person, or anything, the more you will love them for things deeper than what lies on the surface.

Approach your creativity in the same way. Seek to understand it more and more each day. Nurture a deep connection with your craft. Don't settle for a life of barely knowing the depths of your passion. Fall in love with it and rediscover the joy creativity brings.

GO DEEP

The ocean is beautiful. The warm sun caresses your skin. The sand between your toes. The sound of the waves crashing. Whether you're relaxing by the beach, going for a quick swim, or whatever floats your boat (no pun intended), its beauty is undeniable.

But here's the thing. The ocean is beautiful…on the surface.

Strap on some scuba gear, and the fear of the unknown will slowly set in. As you sink into what feels like a bottomless pit, you immediately feel out of place. The pressure kicks in, squeezing every inch of your body. Each breath feels like a luxury. You look up at the surface, drifting further and further away, and in that moment, you regret each decision you made that put you in the situation.

But then, suddenly, something unexpected happens.

A universe of colors explodes around you! You're surrounded by the plethora of unimaginable wildlife you would've never encountered if you stayed relaxing on the surface.

You see vibrant corals, ancient sea turtles, glowing jellyfish, and bioluminescent fish. You explore hidden underwater caves, forests of the sea, and sunken ships. It's truly otherworldly.

You realize the ocean's surface is beautiful, but under the ocean is magical. This is how "knowledge" also works.

As you sink deeper into any topic you start thinking differently and you begin seeing the world through a fresh lens. It's like unlocking a secret chamber in your brain that you didn't even know existed.

Even though we encounter a ton of information daily, we usually appreciate it from a distance, only acknowledging what lies on the surface. But I promise you that the deeper you go, the more magical any subject matter becomes.

I challenge you to go deeper into an aspect of your craft. Force yourself to learn more about it. Learn something that's both "new" and "challenging". Wrestle with its complexities, the things you don't fully understand. Really push yourself, because the areas you find beautiful from afar are filled with more magic than you can ever imagine.

LIFELONG LEARNING

Jim Collins, the author of *Good to Great*, famously wrote, "Good is the enemy of great. We don't have great schools, principally because we have good schools. We don't have great government, principally because we have good government. Few people attain great lives, in large part because it is just so easy to settle for a good life."

Settling for a "good" prevents creators from striving for greatness. Most creators fall into the trap of settling for a "good" skill level, a "good" understanding of the craft, or even a "good" work of art. This mental virus pushes them to stay in their comfort zone. The cure to this virus is remaining a student of your craft. That's never letting yourself fall victim to the comfort of staying in the "good" range. You have to sign a lifelong commitment to learning your craft.

To become a master, you have to understand that mastery isn't a destination. Achieving mastery is a journey. It's a blend of learning, experimenting, and implementing to evolve as your craft constantly evolves. Delve into the origins and evolution of your field. Identify the key creators. Observe their work, process, and career paths to pull insights for your journey. Embrace every learning opportunity with an open mind. Experiment with new methods and technologies. Let your curiosity be your guide.

Key of Influence

"The riches are in the niches."—Pat Flynn

TAYLOR SWIFT

Taylor Swift is an extraordinary artist whose music has touched the hearts and souls of millions across the globe. Her songs have become the voice of her generation, expressing the struggles and joys of life in a way that resonates with her fans.

When Taylor Swift started her career, she loved country music. However, she realized the genre was too broad of an audience. She decided to focus on creating music specifically for teenage girls. Swift's gift for crafting relatable and emotive lyrics for her niche audience set her apart. Drawing on her own experiences with love and heartbreak, she wrote music that spoke directly to her fans.

Swift also researched the intricacies of teen girls' culture and psychology, using her findings to develop a strong brand identity. She spoke their language and leaned into her girly fashion sense and bubbly personality. Embodying these elements allowed each of her fans to see themselves in her.

Swift's success shows how influential creators can become when they dominate a small target audience. Her clearly defined focus enabled her to build a loyal fan base of teenage girls passionate about her music and message. As her popularity grew, she eventually expanded her audience to include other demographics.

THE MAGNIFICENCE OF THE NICHE

A niche audience is a relatively small group of people within the broader population of your industry who share a common interest, passion, or demographic characteristic. Age, gender, geographic location, hobbies, beliefs, and culture are a few factors that can define a niche. They often have unique needs and preferences, and they tend to seek out content, products, and services that cater to their specific interests and desires.

It's common for business owners to say their target market is "everyone," but seasoned entrepreneurs know that trying to acquire the widest market possible will lead to failure. Instead, to build massive businesses, successful entrepreneurs identify and solve a problem for a small niche. Take Warby Parker, for example. This affordable online eyewear company started in 2010, targeting college students looking for stylish glasses. They recognized that many students couldn't afford the high prices of traditional eyewear brands and offered a trendy affordable alternative. This made them the ideal target, and they quickly gained a loyal following in this niche. From there, they expanded to other audiences, such as young professionals and urban residents, while still maintaining their core values of style and affordability. In 2022 Warby Parker's revenue touched $600 million as it continued to be a leading eyewear brand.

Starting with a niche is undoubtedly the best way to spread your creations. Creative geniuses across many fields also use this tactic to grow their audience. Film director Tim Burton is known for creating stories dedicated to his audience of fans who appreciate his quirky, gothic, and dark humor. His films often explore themes of otherness, misfits, and outcasts, which resonate with a niche who may feel like they don't fit in with mainstream society.

Identifying your niche can be challenging. You may feel like you have so much to offer the world that it feels like you're doing your craft a disservice by focusing on a small audience. Don't be tempted to please everyone. Targeting a small but growing group of people with common problems, desires, and interests is the first of many markets you will dominate.

FOLD A SHEET OF PAPER

Let's conduct a thought experiment. Take a regular thin sheet of paper and fold it in half. Then, fold it in half again. And again. Now, the paper would be about as thick as the tip of your fingernail.

But let's take it a step further. Keep folding it in half, over and over again. How thick do you think the paper would be after fifty folds?

This simple exercise illustrates the challenge of comprehending exponential growth for the human brain. As the thickness of the paper doubles with each fold, by the seventh fold, it would already match the thickness of an average notebook. By the tenth fold, it would reach the thickness of your hand. At the seventeenth fold, it would tower over a two-story house. At the thirtieth fold, it would extend to the outer limits of the Earth's atmosphere. And by the fiftieth fold, it would stretch all the way to the Sun.[55]

This fact is just one of many examples of the incredible power of exponential growth. It can be challenging for our brains to grasp, but targeting a niche audience leverages the same mind-boggling

---

[55] Fisk, Peter. 2016. "Demonstrating 'Exponential Growth' by Folding a Sheet of Paper in Half … To the Moon and Beyond!" Peter Fisk. April 24, 2016. https://www.peter fisk.com/2016/04/demonstrating-exponential-growth-by-folding-a-sheet-of-pape r-in-half-to-the-moon-and-beyond/.

effect of folding a sheet of paper fifty times. Niche audiences are a passionate and tightly-knit group, creating an environment where ideas can spread exponentially. In each niche, new information is a key social currency. People share things that make them look good with those they want to impress and fit in with.

If you can strategically package your brand, work, and message and present it to a niche audience effectively, you can ignite a spark that spreads like wildfire. One person shares it with two, then four, then eight, and before you know it, your creations will soar to heights that seem out of this world.

THE 1000 TRUE FANS PRINCIPLE

In 2008, Kevin Kelly, the founding executive editor of *Wired* magazine, wrote a groundbreaking essay that challenged the notion that creators need a massive audience to achieve success. Instead, Kelly argued that all you need are 1000 true fans. He defines true fans as the "ones who will buy everything you produce."[56] They will show up to your shows, be the first people to engage with your new content, and share your work. Essentially, they go the extra mile for you.

The key to success is identifying your niche audience and focusing on deeply connecting with at least 1000 of them. For painters, this could result in selling art prints for $50 each, making $50,000 per collection. For singers, it could mean releasing a song that gets 100,000 streams from a fanbase that listens repeatedly and shares it with others. For YouTubers, it could mean leveraging a loyal fanbase to influence the algorithm and make a video go viral.

Don't underestimate the power of niche audiences. Their passion

---

[56] Kelly, Kevin. 2009. "The Technium: 1,000 True Fans." Kk.org. 2009. https://kk.org/thetechnium/1000-true-fans/.

and ability to spread information quickly can help you reach new heights. By focusing on connecting deeply with a small group of fans, you can build a loyal following that can sustain your work and provide a solid foundation for growth. Find your unique angle, tailor your brand, and connect deeply with your fans.

Key of Recruitment

"If everyone is moving forward together, then success takes care of itself."—Henry Ford

A PAINTER WITHOUT A PAINTBRUSH

Jeff Koons is one of the most wealthy living artists, infamously known for his gimmicky style of art. He pushes the boundaries of traditional art by using visually striking materials and techniques with controversial themes. From bright colors to shiny materials to massive scale, Koons' art embodies pop culture. One of his most notable works, *Rabbit,* a stainless steel sculpture of a rabbit balloon animal, auctioned for over $91 million, making it the most expensive work by a living artist ever sold at auction. Overall, his pieces are diverse. They encompass photography, sculpture, painting, and installation.

The controversy behind Jeff Koons lies beyond the artwork itself. Koons' wealth in the art world reflects his ideas, not his techniques. Koons proudly admits, "I'm basically the 'idea' person. I'm not physically involved in the production." Koons uses a team of highly talented art assistants to bring his ideas to life. He rarely creates the artwork by himself.

His creative process has caused a stir of emotions in the art world. On one side, some argue that Koons' art feels inauthentic, as if he slaps his signature on someone else's work. His work sells for record-breaking prices, yet the artists who created the work receive little compensation. Does it make sense for Jeff Koons to receive all the credit and money from a sale even though he often can't create the work himself?

On the other hand, Jeff Koons arguably plays the role of a creative director. The job of a creative director is to use their knowledge about creativity in their field to generate an overarching idea that a team can create. Most times, the vision for his ideas is so ambitious that it would not be possible for one person to execute it. With his leadership, these ambitious ideas came to fruition. Koons says he plays the role of a director in his process. He uses his knowledge from his time spent at the Maryland Institute College of Art and various tools to create the original idea for his pieces. Then he assembles a team of specialist artists to make it happen. Koons' New York workspace employs over one hundred of the world's most talented artists to bring his ideas to life.

Artists throughout history have employed assistants to bring their visions to life. Andy Warhol's studio, known as The Factory, was a hub of creativity where artists, writers, musicians, and other creatives collaborated. Even in the 16th century, Michelangelo hired assistants to paint the Sistine Chapel. The ethics behind this process still stands as a debate in the art world, but the main lesson to pull from Jeff, Andy, Michelangelo, and other creators is the power of a team. Instead of using a combination of oil paint or pencils as a tool, these artists brought their visions to life by using a combination of people. Many creative geniuses throughout history have used teams to give life to their massive ideas.

IT TAKES A VILLAGE

When Will Smith spoke on his experience behind his success he said, "Who your friends are, who you're with everyday, will make or break your dreams…you probably can't do much of anything in this life at a high level without a rock-solid team." Ideas are like babies. It's conceived in the mind of the creator and nurtured to life with their time, effort, and resources. As time passes, the idea grows and evolves, taking on a life of its own and finding its place in the world in ways you couldn't have predicted. But, like a child, it takes a village to raise an idea. It requires the support and guidance of a community to thrive. An idea's potential lies in the number of people with vested interest in its success. You have to find and partner with exceptional team members who believe in your vision.

Ambitious ideas require an ambitious leader. To harness the potential of an idea, it is necessary to gather a team of exceptional individuals who share your vision. As the great Steve Jobs once said, "Great things in business are never done by one person. They're done by a team of people." Christopher Nolan needs a team of cinema professionals to tell his mind-bending stories. Frank Lloyd Wright, the pioneer of modern architecture, needs a team of builders to make his drafts a reality. Steve Jobs building Apple, Elon Musk building Space X, and Phil Knight building Nike are a few examples of visionary team builders who fought tooth and nail to bring their ideas to life. Their ability to change the world can trace back to their overlapping skill of selling their vision. Creative geniuses understand that at some point they may have to play the role of director to give their ideas the life it deserves. They are aware that successfully executing a massive vision is often a collaborative effort. It takes inspiring a network of individuals with different skill sets, backgrounds, and perspectives to provide the necessary support, feedback, and guidance to bring an idea to fruition. They package their vision into a pitch and use it to recruit the best team members they can.

THE PRODUCT

Creating a product requires a talented workflow. An engineer is tasked with making the product functional, while a seasoned designer establishes the brand. Then it's handed off to the head of operations to figure out how to make the product at scale. Once that's figured out, a marketer executes the best strategy of getting the product in front of all the right people. The individual mastery of skill sets in this team increases the chances of the product's success. This workflow would be flawed without any of them.

Without this collaborative effort, it would take one person ten times longer to launch a product. The lesson here is that oftentimes creative success is not a solo sport. Essentially, you should build a business where you or your ideas are the product. If you want to amplify your reach and achieve greatness in your field, build a quality team.

To see the power of collaboration in action, look at your favorite music artist's album credits. Rarely will you find only the artist's name. Instead, you're going to find the producers who sent their beats back and forth until they perfected them. You'll see co-writers who had a group writing session where one person probably created the hook, another person the melody, and the third person wrote the verses. That's not all. If you continue researching, you will uncover even more people. There's the designer for the album artwork, the manager who kept everyone organized, the audio engineer who mixed the song, and more. Your favorite artist's album is the product of a larger team of people. As dancer-choreographer Twyla Tharp said, "People in a good collaboration accomplish more than the group's most talented members could achieve on their own."

I'm not saying you can't be successful without a team. You can, and I'm sure you will if you try. But I can guarantee you that whatever you accomplish alone is minor compared to having ten other people working alongside you. Even the legendary Michael Jordan said, "Talent wins games, but teamwork and intelligence win championships." Teams take you beyond your potential.

THE TWO MOST IMPORTANT TEAM TRAITS

Over a decade, Google conducted a data study called Aristotle.[57] They spent millions of dollars tracking 180 teams. Google's goal was to discover the common traits of the highest-performing teams. They hypothesized that matching personality types and the group's overall likability was the key to success. They were wrong. The study revealed two specific behaviors that all the most effective teams shared.

The first is called "equality in distribution of conversational turn-taking." Each team member over the years, on average, spoke for roughly the same amount of time. Depending on the task, leadership shifted from teammate to teammate based on their strengths, yet everyone valued each other's input. Simply put, if everyone in the group got a chance to talk, the team excelled. Each person speaking allowed ideas to evolve.

The second group trait they discovered was a "high average social sensitivity." The team members could infer how others felt based on body language cues like tone of voice or facial expressions. When they tested all the teams, the best teams scored above average. A team with a high average social sensitivity can read a room and notice if someone is feeling left out of a brainstorming session and pull

---

[57] Coding Tech. 2018. "Secrets of Successful Teamwork: Insights from Google." YouTube Video. YouTube. https://www.youtube.com/watch?v=hHIikHJV9fI.

them into the conversation to get their input. They understand each other's perspectives and openly discuss ideas without bringing their team members down. According to Harvard Business Review, "high-performing teams deliver roughly five times as many positive statements (supportive, appreciative, encouraging) to every one negative statement (critical, disapproving, contradictory)."

Both of these traits fall under the umbrella of psychological safety. Ideas thrive in environments where people feel safe sharing their thoughts. Use the results of this study to assemble a team that's talented and respectful of each other's minds.

BIRDS OF A FEATHER

History has shown that creative geniuses usually cluster in the same cities at the same time. Plato, Socrates, Pericles, and Thucydides were all in Athens around 300 BC. Michelangelo, Leonardo da Vinci, and Donatello were all in Florence in the mid 1400s. Shakespeare, Marlowe, and Nashe were all in London in the early 1600s. Paris in the early 20th century housed figures like Pablo Picasso, Ernest Hemingway, Gertrude Stein, F. Scott Fitzgerald, and Salvador Dalí. In the 1920s, The Harlem Renaissance spread as New York City became a cultural center for African American writers, artists, musicians, and thinkers including Langston Hughes, Zora Neale Hurston, and Duke Ellington. Silicon Valley in the late 20th century had a concentration of new technological innovators and entrepreneurs like Steve Jobs, Larry Page, and Sergey Brin. In every creative industry you will find this phenomenon of creative geniuses gathering to feed off of each other's energy.

Your number one goal for building a team should be partnering with people you admire. Motivational speaker Jim Rohn famously said that we are the average of the five people we spend the most time with. You are influenced the most by the people you spend the most time with—your behaviors, interests, mood, thoughts, self-esteem, decisions, and inevitably your success. Choose wisely.

Surround yourself with people you admire, amplify your reach, and share your ideas. After identifying the roles you need to fill, craft your vision in a clear and compelling pitch. Use stories or visuals to convey your idea. Find people who fill the role and fit the mold of valuable team traits and pitch them on your vision. Open an invitation for them to join your team. Together you can change the world.

* * *

Did any of these keys spark an interesting thought?
Share it with me at WorldOfCreatives.com

Key of Obsession

"Obsessed is a word the lazy use to describe the dedicated."—Russell Warren Howe

MOZART

Wolfgang Amadeus Mozart was different from your average music child prodigy. Instead of being naturally musically inclined, he worked tirelessly to understand and master the craft. His father noticed Mozart's interest at a young age and endlessly fed his curiosity. He taught Mozart all the fundamentals of music and surrounded him with talented music composers in Europe. By the time Mozart was six years old, he had already composed his first symphony.

As Mozart grew older, his love of music intensified. Mozart created operas, concertos, symphonies, and sonatas that shaped classical music as we know it. In his short thirty-five years of life, he composed more than 600 works, many acknowledged as pinnacles of Western music. How did he find the time to master his craft and create so many legendary works? Well, the secret lies in his daily routine. In a letter to his sister written in 1782, Mozart outlines a typical day in his life:

"At six o'clock in the morning I have my hair dressed, and have finished my toilet by seven o'clock. I write till nine. From nine

to one I give lessons. I then dine, unless I am invited out, when dinner is usually at two o'clock, sometimes at three, as it was today, and will be tomorrow at Countess Zichi's and Countess Thun's. I cannot begin to work before five or six o'clock in the evening, and I am often prevented doing so by some concert; otherwise I write till nine o'clock. I then go to my dear Constanze, though our pleasure in meeting is frequently embittered by the unkind speeches of her mother, which I will explain to my father in my next letter. Thence comes my wish to liberate and rescue her as soon as possible. At half-past ten or eleven I go home, but this depends on the mother's humor, or on my patience in bearing it. Owing to the number of concerts, and also the uncertainty whether I may not be summoned to one place or another, I cannot rely on my evening writing, so it is my custom (especially when I come home early) to write for a time before going to bed. I often sit up writing till one, and rise again at six."

This letter was one of many written accounts of Mozart's rigorous daily routine. On average, he spent twelve hours a day engulfed in music. By the time he was twenty-eight years old, his hands were deformed because of all the hours he dedicated to practicing, studying, performing, teaching, and composing. Mozart was obsessed, often to the detriment of his health and social life. He willingly worked harder than most creators to become a master. Mozart was a well-rounded musician who wrote compositions for all instruments in all combinations. "People err who think my art comes easily to me," he wrote to a friend. "I assure you, dear friend, nobody has devoted so much time and thought to composition as I. There is not a famous master whose music I have not industriously studied through many times."

Mozart's life was filled with pain and turmoil, but his love of music never wavered. He continued to compose and perform, even on his deathbed. As a result of his obsession, he left a legacy of some of the most beautiful and influential music in history. We remember him as one of the greatest composers of all time.

BALANCING ACT

You will rarely find a legendary creator who wasn't obsessed. When someone is obsessed with something, it takes up all of their time. Imagine how talented a pianist would be if they practiced for four hours a day. After years of practice, they would be able to play complex pieces and execute challenging compositions with precision. They would effortlessly convey emotions comfortably and confidently in front of large audiences.

Now, that's the after-effect of four hours of practice a day. Mozart practiced twelve hours a day. That's three of this imaginary pianist's lives packed into one person. That's the power of obsession. It unlocks your ability to give your craft the accumulation of multiple lives. When people say that someone's talents are ahead of their time, it's usually a result of them being so deeply passionate about their idea, craft, or pursuit that they find themselves completely immersed in it for a significant period. The combination of curiosity and time commitment enables them to explore every element and push the boundaries of what's humanly possible.

While obsession can be a powerful tool for unlocking creativity, the dangers of obsession occur when we push ourselves too far. It can result in deteriorating your health, social life, and even your creativity. It can lead to creative burnout, a mental state where you lack the energy, motivation, and inspiration to do anything. To avoid this state, you have to be aware of your limits and take breaks to give your mind and body what it needs to rejuvenate. Writer Audre Lorde wrote extensively about the importance of self-care and rest to prevent creative burnout, stating that "caring for myself is not self-indulgence, it is self-preservation." Also, obsession can cause you to neglect other important areas of life. For example, Michael Jackson dedicated his entire life to his craft. His intense focus on music led him to neglect his physical health, have distant relationships with loved ones, and regret missing out on his childhood.

THE PRICE OF OBSESSION

It's crucial to be aware of the upsides and downsides of obsession because it comes at a price. You can't buy the benefits of obsession with money. You pay for it with your focus. Your level of obsession is the accumulation of time you spend laser-focused on your craft. When you commit to focusing on becoming a master for hours a day, you drastically increase your odds of accomplishing your goals. A proverb illustrates this well: "If a hungry fox chases two rabbits, both will escape."

OPPORTUNITY COST

In microeconomics, there's a concept called opportunity cost. The opportunity cost is the cost of your choices. Each choice you make costs you all the other options you didn't choose. For example, if you go to the movies, you cannot spend the money you spent on the movie ticket on something else. Time is also a factor. You could've spent those two hours reading a book, bonding with your mom, or relaxing in bed.

As we navigate our lives, we perpetually transact value. You're not constantly spending money, but you're always spending time. Right now, you're reading this book at the cost of reading someone else's book. The value you're getting from the time you spend reading this book is what you gain in exchange for the opportunity cost of everything else you could've been doing. Thank you for your time.

The good news is that reading this book is time spent on your craft. It's leveling up your obsession. You have to figure out what level you're comfortable with. Right now, you could be grabbing something to eat, exercising, or spending time with your loved ones. That's what you're sacrificing right now to obsess over your craft.

Before you drop my book and run to spend time with your family, let me remind you that you need to find your balance. You can't spend all your time eating, in the gym, or with your family. You have to take this currency and strategize how you want to spend the 86,400 seconds you get each day. Some creators are comfortable with straying into the deep end of obsession, stealing them away from everything else. Constanze Mozart was Wolfgang Mozart's wife and loyal companion until he died in 1791. In the letter he sent to his sister above, he mentioned that he only spent two hours with her a day. That's twelve hours with music and two hours with the love of his life. You need to find your balance. Is reading this book right now worth it? How much do you want your craft to bleed into your personal life? Find that line, and promise yourself that you'll never cross it.

BALANCE

Beyoncé is an undeniable creative genius. There aren't enough pages in this book to go into the depths of what makes her a once-in-a-lifetime spectacle. My personal experience at her *Renaissance* tour offered a live testament to creativity in its purest form.

Her behind-the-scenes documentary solidified everything I felt. She revealed how she leveraged all the resources at her disposal to amplify her creative vision. Every single detail of her concert was meticulously considered.

She spent four years developing her tour. She crafted a vision and message she wanted to share with the world and brought together a team of creators to help her bring it to life. She inspired them to transcend their perceived limits.

She iterated on hundreds of stage designs, lighting arrangements, and visual elements to create an environment that encapsulated her trailblazing music. Each show's attire was a bold fashion statement. When she took the stage, she commanded the audience's attention. Her blend of choreography and angelic voice was surreal. She showcased what a master performer looked like.

This is the level of obsession it takes to solidify your essence as a creative genius. But there's one more thing that makes Beyoncé special. One of the aspects of Beyoncé that I admire most is that in all of her greatness as a creator, she managed to maintain an equally great relationship with her family. She found balance. If Beyoncé, the Queen Bee, can find balance in all she accomplishes, so can you.

YOU ARE WHAT YOU THINK

When people are obsessed over their craft, it's what they think and talk about all day. They can't get it out of their head. They're constantly processing how their art relates to the ever-changing world around them. Eventually, they become their thoughts. Ralph Waldo Emerson once said, "You become what you think about all day long." It's why you can't discuss Jazz without talking about Miles Davis, Pop Art without Andy Warhol, or basketball without Michael Jordan. These creators' obsession with their craft made them synonymous with it.

You can be successful in your field without being obsessed. But some creators want more than success. They want to leave a mark on the craft as a whole for generations to come. If you want to go down in history as a legend in your field, you must be deeply obsessed. You may live a personal life of hell, and you may not even live to see the fruits of your labor, but you will have a human experience like no other. You will achieve depths in your craft that humans won't experience for decades to come. You will truly fall in love with your craft to the point where you'll be lying on your deathbed, happily creating your last creation.

Key of Practice

BRUCE LEE

Bruce Lee is one of the most influential martial artists and entertainers of all time. His films and performances popularized Asian martial arts in the West, inspiring a generation of filmmakers and action stars. His impact on pop culture is indisputable. Dana White, UFC President, called Lee the "father of mixed martial arts," and *TIME* named him one of the hundred most influential people of the 20th century.

Bruce Lee surpassed the skillset of his opponents by approaching his craft with philosophies. These philosophies dictated how he navigated life and martial arts. Some included ideas that implemented flow into his craft. Others were about the importance of learning and how to approach it. Many of these philosophies helped him perfect his martial arts techniques. Lee used all of his philosophies as guidelines and stayed within his rules. Eventually, Bruce Lee developed a unique style of martial arts called Jeet Kune Do.

Jeet Kune Do is known as an "intelligent martial art." Bruce Lee formed it from his fighting techniques combined with philosophical influence from Eclecticism, Zen Buddhism, and Taoism. He believed that Jeet Kune Do was a way of life, a mental and spiritual discipline in addition to physical practice. This blend of the mind, body, and soul was Lee's method of making martial arts a holistic craft.

BRUCE LEE'S CORE PHILOSOPHY

Like most creative geniuses, Bruce Lee kept a notebook and recorded his training regime and philosophical thoughts. His writings revealed a key trait that helped him become a legend in martial arts, saying, "A self-willed man has no other aim than his own growth. He values only one thing, the mysterious power in himself, which bids him live and helps him to grow. His only living destiny is the silent, ungainsayable law in his own heart, which comfortable habits make it so hard to obey but which the self-willed man is destiny and godhead."

Lee valued the power of being self-willed. A self-willed creative person doesn't wait for inspiration to practice. They set a schedule and practice even when they feel unmotivated or not in the mood. A self-willed creator stays focused on their inner power to dictate their growth and development. This belief becomes the guiding principle of their success. It gives them the ultimate authority over their own life.

James Clear, the author of *Atomic Habits*, wrote in his blog about the importance of creative people having a schedule saying, "Stop waiting for motivation or creative inspiration to strike you and set a schedule for your habits. This is the difference between professionals and amateurs. Professionals set a schedule and stick to it. Amateurs wait until they feel inspired or motivated." It will take a long time for you to achieve mastery, so don't let the world around you dictate the amount of time you spend on your craft.

10,000-HOUR RULE

In Malcolm Gladwell's book *Outliers: The Story of Success*, he talks about a research study on the habits and practice routines of elite performers in sports, music, chess, and more. The research found that it takes around 10,000 hours of focused practice for people to achieve mastery in their field.

Thomas Edison's quote, "Genius is 1% inspiration and 99% perspiration," embodies the 10,000-hour rule. You can only unlock your creative potential if you dedicate the quality time needed to perfect your craft. The time it takes to become a master elevates mastery from being a relaxing hobby to a committed lifestyle. To put it in perspective, you have to build a habit of practicing for almost three hours a day for ten years to reach 10,000 hours.

INFINITE GAME

Simon Sinek popularized a concept called The Infinite Game. An infinite game is a game you play where conventional rules don't apply. Instead of playing to win like a typical game, the goal of an infinite game is to keep on playing.

Creativity is an infinite game. The primary focus is the process of creation, rather than a final product. It doesn't follow set rules or fixed boundaries. You create the rules. And along the way, you have to engage in a continuous process of exploration and innovation if you want to keep playing because creativity evolves over time as new ideas, styles, and expressions constantly emerge. To continue playing you must commit to growing continuously.

THE PARETO PRINCIPLE

The Pareto Principle, also known as the 80/20 rule, is a principle that suggests that 80% of the results come from 20% of the causes. Economist Vilfredo Pareto coined the term when he observed that 20% of the Italian population owned 80% of the wealth in Italy. Since then, it has shown in many other ways. 20% of the world's population owns 80% of the wealth, 20% of criminals commit 80% of crimes, and 80% of the public uses 20% of their computers' features.

The Pareto Principle is why Bruce Lee once said, "I fear not the man who has practiced 10,000 kicks once, but I fear the man who has practiced one kick 10,000 times." Here, Lee addresses the advantage of focused practice. His advice is against generally practicing dancing, tennis, or the drums. Instead, he's saying that you need to identify the fundamental dance routines, racket swings, or drum patterns and practice them relentlessly. Practice it daily for hours until it becomes second nature. That's how you practice the 20% of tactics that make up 80% of mastery. Spend 80% of your time practicing those tactics and 20% experimenting with others. By identifying these key elements and focusing on them first, you can make more progress in less time.

If you practice the wrong or unnecessary techniques, you will improve, but you will fall behind others in your field who deliberately practiced the most impactful things. The only way to know the right moves to practice is by continuously studying the masters and their tactics. Keep an open mind, but carefully filter through the advice you receive on adjusting your practice. Your creative mastery depends on it.

FORGE YOUR PATH

When you try something new for the first time, neurons in your brain start making new connections. Your neural pathways work similarly to walking through a field of tall grass. The first time you try, it's rough and blinding, and you might not get to your destination the first time, but something magical happens when you come back every day to try again. Eventually, the repetitive hiking will forge a beaten pathway through the grass where you'll be able to head to your destination effortlessly.

You have to commit to walking the pathways of your craft daily. Everyone's path is different, but you can discover the best path to take by studying the creative geniuses of your field. What techniques did they use? What fundamentals did they abide by? What mistakes have they made that you should avoid? These are all the elements that make up their pathway to mastery. Use it as your guide. Remember, it will take thousands of hours of deliberate focus to forge your path to mastery, but once you get there, you will be free to explore uncharted territories of your craft that fellow creators can only dream of.

Key of Commitment

"Success is the sum of small efforts, repeated day in and day out."—Robert Collier

PREDICTING THE FUTURE

As creators, we often dream of that one breakthrough moment when our work catapults us to success. We envision the standing ovation at our art show, the glowing reviews of our debut album, or the rocketship growth of our business after launch. While you should treasure these moments, they don't hold the key to our success. Instead, your success is a manifestation of what's constantly happening inside you, your habits, choices, and actions.

Predicting the future is impossible, but you can shape your creative destiny by integrating creativity into your daily routine. Your habits and rituals have the power to direct the trajectory of your life. Your life is the accumulation of these countless moments weaved into countless days. In these seemingly insignificant moments, the essence of your future lies dormant, awaiting your conscious attention. The small choices you make day in and day out, the seemingly mundane habits you cultivate, possess a profound influence on your creative goals, dreams, and desires.

THE POWER OF COMMITMENT

Commitment is the most transformative trait you can implement to change your life. Once you identify the actions required to reach your goals and dreams, you can ignore the worries of the future and the insecurities of the past and focus on making the most out of the path you chose. When you commit in the face of failure, despair, and pain, you will inevitably flourish. This applies to committing to people, a process, and your craft.

Commitment is the bridge between being an ordinary creator and becoming an extraordinary one. The most successful creators have the discipline to create a plan for who they want to become and what they want to create and commit to it, day in and day out. They evolve from being a "creator" to being "creative." It's no longer a title; it's a way of life. Integrate creativity into your daily routine, and you will soar. The longer you commit, the deeper you go. The deeper you go, the more surprising things you will learn about yourself, your craft, and your environment.

TIPPING POINT

In Malcolm Gladwell's book titled *The Tipping Point: How Little Things Can Make a Big Difference*, he discusses a concept coined by sociologist Mark Granovetter in the 1970s called "tipping point." The tipping point is the critical moment before an idea, trend, or behavior rapidly spreads, leading to significant and often unforeseen changes. Gladwell spends the entire book explaining the mysterious power of the tipping point and how it applies to the world around you.

Popular memes spread among a small group of people until it reaches a tipping point and quickly becomes a global sensation. Social movements like #MeToo, LGBTQ+, BLM, and Climate Change

Activism gained momentum through various tipping points that led to significant societal changes. New technological innovations start limited, but it eventually reaches a tipping point when the technology improves, prices decrease, and a substantial number of people embrace their benefits and convenience, leading to rapid global adoption. Mix the ingredients, effort and time, and anything in the universe will experience the unwavering power of the tipping effect.

SLOWLY BUT ALL AT ONCE

Time is limited, and commitment is a contract with yourself on how you plan on allocating your time. How you spend each day will determine the rest of your life. The mind-boggling part is you won't even perceive your daily progress. Change happens slowly and then all at once. It's like a calm river slowly chipping away at a landscape until it grows into roaring waters that carve a massive canyon. The seeds of transformation are sown in the quiet moments of effort, persistence, and dedication. They germinate beneath the surface, hidden from sight, as we toil away day by day.

Then, one day, the tipping point happens, the moment when all the effort starts to show. The culmination of our daily labor alters the landscape of our lives forever. The changes will be strikingly noticeable, not only to you but to the world around you, family, friends, and coworkers. The change will seem sudden because the timing of your tipping point is unpredictable. The great part of commitment is your tipping point is guaranteed. It will come eventually. Use the inevitability of achieving your tipping point as motivation to keep pushing when you're doubting your progress. Trust the process.

On your path to reaching your creative potential, you will encounter many tipping points. At each point, you're going to transform into a new, more expressive creator. Your consistency will result in a leap forward in skill or a sudden breakthrough idea. Your transformation will unlock a greater sense of understanding and intuition of your craft, effortless creativity, and improved creative output. You will step back from your easel in awe, close your eyes and get lost in the melody of your piano strokes, and write epic stories in a fraction of your usual time. The beautiful part of all of this is you're not experiencing a temporary high. You're experiencing your new baseline, a point of no return. Wave goodbye to the old-you and say hello to the present-you, the person you once only dreamed of becoming.

Key of Imagination

"Everything you can imagine is real."—Pablo Picasso

DAVID BLAINE

David Blaine is a renowned magician and performer known for his ability to push the limits of human perception. Blaine's creative genius lies in his ability to craft illusions that leave his audience spellbound. He was four years old when he saw his first magic trick. That sparked a lifelong commitment to becoming one of the best illusionists to walk this earth. At nineteen years old, he gained popularity for his street magic performances scoring him an ABC special called *David Blaine: Street Magic*. Through the camera lens, he was able to captivate the minds of people worldwide. As his popularity grew, so did his feats. He transitioned from performing illusions to taking on real-life stunts. David Blaine was buried alive, held his breath underwater for 17 minutes and 4 seconds, and lived in a block of ice for over 63 hours.

David Blaine has a show in Vegas where he demonstrates his mastery of blending imagination with reality. His performances are a seamless journey into his mind. He often builds up to the climax of his tricks through a series of minor illusions or stunts. He uses stories, props, and verbal and physical cues to misdirect your attention and create illusions that are indistinguishable from reality.

Why does our mind allow us to believe and experience things we know aren't real? Search for "the rubber hand experiment"[58] on YouTube, and you will see a clear answer. In this experiment, researchers trick the participant's brains into believing a rubber hand is a real part of their body. Achieving this illusion was easy. All they did was place the rubber hand next to their real hand and then stroke both hands in unison with a brush. Eventually, the participants started to imagine they could feel the brushing sensation on the rubber hand. The experiment ends when the researcher slams the rubber hand with a hammer, causing the participant to jump in pain as if they hit their hand. Yes, a few strokes of a feather on a rubber hand is enough for your imagination to take the wheel of your reality. Our minds have the incredible ability to blur the line between what we imagine and what's real, allowing us to experience things that we know aren't real.

David Blaine's shows in Vegas are a testament to the power of perception and the art of deception. Fans from all over the world travel to witness his incredible feats and embark on a journey into the depths of their own minds. Blaine's performances allow us to suspend our disbelief and bend the nature of our existence for just a moment, reminding us of the magic and wonder that lies within us all.

IMAGINARY FRIENDS

The source and purpose of imagination remain a mystery, but one thing is clear: we are all born with a powerful imagination. For some children, this imaginative prowess is a constant 24/7 activity, as Christopher Moore noted when he said, "Children see magic because they look for it." The world they live in is vastly more unique and

---

[58] "The Rubber Hand Illusion - Horizon: Is Seeing Believing? - BBC Two." n.d. Www.youtube.com. https://www.youtube.com/watch?v=sxwn1w7MJvk.

curiosity-inducing than ours. They freely burst out in play, pretending to live out various career paths, embody other species, and develop superpowers.

As a child, our imaginations are unhinged. Yet, as we grow up, it becomes stifled and suppressed. This is a shame because research has shown that children with imaginary friends are more creative, have an advanced vocabulary, and are better able to empathize and understand the thoughts and feelings of others. In fact, imaginative kids are more likely to grow up into creative adults, as their knack for free thinking stays with them throughout their lives.

This correlation suggests that cultivating our imagination can lead to greater creativity. The key difference between your average genius and a creative genius is that the former has expert knowledge of a particular field, while the latter has a boundless imagination. Take pianist Barry Harris, for example. He spent his time thinking about and testing unique ways to break the rules of music. His applied curiosity led him to invent an entirely new piano scale called The 6th Diminished Scale, solidifying himself as a creative genius.

Typically, scientists study the depths of current knowledge and build on top of those facts. They often rely on data to guide their research, but when they tap into their imagination, they come up with theories that, if proven, can shake the truth of the universe. That's what made Albert Einstein so special. He frequently acknowledged the power of imagination and leveraged it in his scientific pursuits. He once said, "I am enough of an artist to draw freely upon my imagination. Imagination is more important than knowledge. Knowledge is limited. Imagination encircles the world."

THE WORLD IS A CANVAS

The transformative power of imagination is truly remarkable. When you exercise your imagination it changes your mind. When you utilize your imagination it changes the world. When we dive into the depths of imaginative thought, we briefly escape reality and come face to face with endless possibilities. I say "possibilities" because that's exactly what it is—possible. Whatever you imagine is one of the infinite possibilities of what reality can become.

For the most part, we are already living in the realized imaginations of other humans. One way to tell if something is a product of thought is to ask yourself this: is there a point in human history when this thing didn't exist? If the answer is yes, then it's not objectively real; it's subjectively real. It's a shared imagination.

Your favorite sport is an idea. So is our favorite movie. Also, the rules you follow and the government that makes them. Your job position, the money you earn, and the goods you purchase are all products of thought. Every idea, invention, and discovery began as a thought in someone's mind. They all trace back to an idea that spawned from the imagination of a past human, someone who saw a vision of how the world could be.

But here's the thing: you, too, have the power to imagine and create new realities. Your imagination is like a brush, and the world is your canvas. With it, you can invent new products, technologies, and systems that can transform how we all live and interact with the world. So don't be afraid to let your mind wander and dream big. The possibilities are truly infinite, and you never know what kind of world-changing idea might be hiding in your imagination.

PAINTING THE WORLD'S CANVAS

To an artist, a blank canvas is both exciting and daunting. It's a playground with infinite potential outcomes waiting to be created. Out of the limitless options, an artist can only choose one. The world, as we perceive it, works the same way. It's a blank canvas with infinite possibilities. Other than the naturally evolving universe, the world is constantly changing based on the ideas we paint on it.

As Lewis Carroll once said, "Imagination is our most powerful tool in the war against reality." It's up to us as creators to pull people into our imagination and shift their perception of the world. If you can do this at scale, you will change the world. You are the bridge between your imaginary world and the real world. Imagine a reality and fight for its existence.

The only thing standing between your imagination and reality is self-doubt. If you don't believe your ideas are achievable, they will never see the light of day. Believe in your creative potential. Trust that your ability to imagine it already makes it possible. George Bernard Shaw put it beautifully, saying, "Imagination is the beginning of creation. You imagine what you desire, you will what you imagine, and at last, you create what you will." So paint the world with the vibrant colors of your imagination.

* * *

Did any of these keys spark an interesting thought?
Share it with me at WorldOfCreatives.com

Key of Leadership

"In leading a team of people, the focus is on efficiency and productivity. In leading a team of creative people, the focus is on exploration and discovery."—Richard Florida

STEVE JOBS

Nothing is more powerful than a well-oiled team of creatives working together to achieve a common goal. Even seemingly impossible visions can come to life with all hands on deck. The largest roadblock your creative team will face in their success is highly dependent on the quality of you, their leader.

When it comes to great leaders, Steve Jobs immediately springs to mind. Steve Jobs is the founder of Apple, the world's first trillion-dollar company. Forged in the image of its founder, many of Apple's most recognized consumer technology products are a direct result of Steve's radical creative leadership style. Even years after he passed in 2011, his ideologies continue to echo through Apple's culture and innovations.

What set Steve Jobs apart from other leaders was the type of people he was capable of leading. He had the ability to inspire and guide the kind of people who don't fit neatly into corporate structures. Creative types march to the beat of their own drum and can be difficult to manage. They're usually the outcasts in the office. Steve's leadership principles were perfect for rallying the most brilliant creative thinkers, dreamers, and rule-breakers to collaborate on one shared vision.

In an interview he said, "The greatest people are self-managing. They don't need to be managed. Once they know what to do, they'll go figure out how to do it. They don't need to be managed at all. What they need is a common vision, and that's what leadership is. What leadership is is having a vision, being able to articulate that so the people around you can understand it, and getting a consensus on a common vision. We wanted people that were insanely great at what they did, but were not necessarily those seasoned professionals, but who had in the tips of their fingers and in their passion, the latest understanding of where technology was and what we could do with that technology, and who wanted to bring that to lots of people. So the neatest thing that happens is when you get a core group of 10 great people, it becomes self-policing as to who they let into that group. So I consider the most important job of someone like myself is recruiting."

Most creative people are scattered with their goals and ideas, pushing companies away from hiring them. But as advertising legend David Ogilvy once said, "The best way to manage creative people is to let them be creative." Steve Jobs did just that. He let them be creative but acted as a constant reminder of the company's goals. He infused freedom, hard work, and experimentation into his team, but when they started to veer off in the wrong direction, he aggressively got them back on track.

YOUR ROLE AS A LEADER

Creators lined up to follow Steve Jobs because they admired his creative genius. People wanted to be like him and contribute to his ambitious visions for Apple. True leadership is not telling others what to do. It's inspiring them to be their best selves. That's why to thrive as a creative leader you have to lead by example.

Become the creator who has the power to inspire others to dream more, learn more, do more, and become more. If you slack off on self-growth, your team will know. It will show in the lackluster ideas you share and the uninspiring stories you tell. When you relentlessly exercise and improve your creativity, you will demonstrate to your team that it's possible to turn an idea into reality.

Creativity is more than coming up with great ideas. It's also about the process of bringing those ideas to life. As a creative leader, you must understand the creative process and how to manage it effectively. You have to know when to step in and provide guidance and when to step back and let your team take the lead. You have to be able to balance the need for structure and direction with the need for freedom and flexibility.

To do this, you have to wear multiple hats. Sometimes you play the role of a leader who is solely orchestrating the creative process. Other times you have to not only participate in the process but also confidently contribute top-tier ideas. This means challenging your team to reach their full potential, as well as being willing to listen and learn to improve on their ideas. As Gary Hamel put it, "Leading a team of creative people requires you to be both a coach and a player." You have to be Phil Knight and Michael Jordan.

TRUST AND RESPONSIBILITY

Steve Jobs was never afraid to take risks. His fearlessness inspired his team to think outside the box and take risks in their own work. As a creative leader, it's important to remember that the creative process is not linear. It's not a straightforward path from idea to finished product. The process is often messy, unpredictable, and sometimes frustrating.

One of the toughest parts about leading a team of creators is you are going to confront unusual challenges because you're pursuing unusual goals. As creators, we often operate in uncharted territories. While this can be exhilarating, it comes with guaranteed setbacks and failures. These struggles can discourage your team from following through to the end. An essential aspect of creative leadership is creating a culture of experimentation and risk-taking. To do this, great creative leaders take on the responsibility for the team's failures while praising them for their successes. Arnold H. Glasow described this leadership principle saying, "A good leader takes a little more than his share of the blame, a little less than his share of the credit."

When Elon Musk was leading SpaceX's team to provide a lower-cost alternative for launching small payloads into orbit, their first rocket, the Falcon 1, failed on its first three attempts to reach orbit. The criticism poured in, but Elon Musk took all the blame. After each failure, he met with the team to learn and adapt. These lessons ultimately led to the fourth launch successfully reaching orbit in 2008.

Elite creative thinkers will dedicate their time and energy to work on your ambitious ideas if they trust you will do everything in your power to fulfill the vision. Your team's goals should keep you up at night because the execution of your ideas could determine the trajectory of the rest of their careers. Not every idea you have will be a success, but that's okay if you take full accountability and focus on learning from your mistakes.

FUELING YOUR TEAM'S GROWTH

Creative people hate to feel stagnant. In the traditional work environment, once a person settles into their role, most of their work becomes routine, repetitive tasks. That's the creator's worst nightmare. If you lead a team of creators, they'll crave new opportunities to grow in their craft. They are driven by their desire to push boundaries and challenge the status quo.

As a leader, it's your responsibility to help your team members break out of this cycle and discover new ways to express their creativity. Push them beyond their perceived limitations. Encourage them to explore their passions. Point them to explore new ways to approach their projects. It's not just about giving them the freedom to learn. It's also about providing them with the resources and support they need to succeed. These include access to new technology or tools, training opportunities, or mentorship programs. Remember, leadership isn't about building a following; it's about empowering others to become leaders themselves.

Many leaders think that empowering their team takes away from their shine. Leave your ego at the door. Leadership isn't about power. It's about building a tight-knit community of top-notch creators that can blossom beyond executing your ideas. It's bigger than you. When you focus on developing leaders, you're contributing to a brighter future for all of humanity. Plus, this is a mutually beneficial principle. It's like taking care of a garden. If you water them diligently and give the plants the sunlight they need, they will reap fruitful creations. The measure of a master gardener isn't the number of seeds they plant; it's the number of fruits they harvest.

Key of Mentorship

"It doesn't matter what you know if you can't teach it."—Mike Holmgren

SHAWN "JAY Z" CARTER

Shawn Carter, popularly known as Jay Z, burst into the limelight with his 1996 debut album *Reasonable Doubt*. Since then, he has released twenty-three studio albums, including collaborative albums with other artists such as Kanye West, Beyoncé, and more. What's even more impressive is that Jay Z built an empire of his brands spread across several industries. He founded Rocawear, a fashion retailer, Tidal, a music streaming service, Roc Nation, an entertainment agency, and Monogram, a line of cannabis products, to name a few. In 2019, Jay Z's business acumen solidified him in music history as the first hip-hop billionaire.

A critical part of his success, in his own words, was mentorship. Jay Z's first mentor was Jaz-O, also known as The Originator. He showed him the inner workings of the music industry and gave him his first big break. At each major milestone of his meteoric rise to power, Jay Z learned from mentors. His mentors' impact instilled his value of the mentor-mentee relationship.

He touched on the importance of mentorship in an interview, saying,

"Most people that were successful growing up from where I was from never came back. So there was never a dialogue on, 'How'd you do it? What happened?'. There was no mentoring program. There was no going back and grabbing a person and teaching them a trade or, you know, what it is that you do. And then that person goes back and grabs two people, and then, you know, it grows from there." For Jay Z, mentorship became a personal responsibility. It was an avenue for personal growth in his community.

Jay Z approached mentoring the same way others mentored him. He hand-selected mentees he saw potential in. His mentorship aided the success of J. Cole, Rihanna, Kanye, and many more superstars. When Jay Z took Kanye under his wing, he showed him how to turn his ego into a superpower. He also helped Rihanna make her first album, *Music of the Sun*. He taught both of them that their craft is more than music. It's a business. Now, like their mentor, Kanye and Rihanna are self-made billionaires from building businesses out of their brands. Jay Z solidified his title as a creative genius by identifying and nurturing creative geniuses. He taught them while simultaneously learning from them. These strategic relationships grew his influence, power, and creative potential.

THE RESPONSIBILITY

There's a major risk you take on by being a mentor. Take note of this: the mentor-mentee relationship is one of the most vulnerable human relationships. It's even more vulnerable than a therapist-patient relationship. When a mentee comes to a mentor for big life decisions, they will aimlessly follow anything a mentor advises them to do. A mentor can influence their mentee's ideas about the world. It can completely shift the trajectory of their entire life. A mentor's advice has the ability to change their mentee at their core. Be extremely careful and intentional in this relationship. If you don't have advice that's based on a proven track record, admit your ignorance instead of sharing an opinion.

REFLECTION

What if whenever you saw one of your friends, they recommended a new movie? If you watch five of them and they all had boring plots, dense characters, and uninspiring visuals, you're going to stop listening to your friend's recommendations. Even if those were the only five movies they ever said were horrible, you would never watch any more of their recommendations. Those five movies become a reflection of their entire taste in film.

A mentor-mentee relationship works the same way. Your mentee's success is a reflection of you. It can magnify the reach and power of your creativity beyond measure, but it can also swallow your entire personal brand.

Lil Wayne is my favorite music artist of all time and a true creative genius. He is crafty with his word choice, masterful at storytelling, and experimental with his flow. He doesn't remember much of his songs because many of his greatest hits were moments in the studio where he was freestyle rapping for fun. Yet he managed to spontaneously create some of the most clever lyrics ever spoken. Years after listening to his songs on repeat, I still manage to discover hidden lyrical gems that previously flew over my head.

When Lil Wayne introduced the world to Nicki Minaj and Drake, his cosign led to two of the greatest artists of all time. Lil Wayne's style and approach to rap profoundly impacted their music. You can hear Lil Wayne's influence in Drake and Nicki Minaj's unique flow, wordplay, and use of punchlines and metaphors in their lyrics. They've also cited Lil Wayne as an inspiration in terms of his work ethic and dedication to the craft of rap. Lil Wayne's ability to acknowledge and nurture true artistry elevated society's respect for his art. Now, Lil Wayne, Nicki Minaj, and Drake create in a league of their own.

THE FEYNMAN TECHNIQUE

Richard Feynman, Nobel Laureate and theoretical physicist, created a deep learning technique called the Feynman Technique. Feynman used this method to solidify his understanding of complicated concepts in modern physics.

It's very difficult to explain complex ideas in a simple, elegant way. The Feynman Technique exercises this muscle. It focuses on using the simple aspects of a topic to help build a deep understanding.

To apply this technique, pick a topic from your craft and teach it to someone else in the simplest way possible. Don't use big, fancy industry-standard words. Break down the concepts and techniques into basic steps that a novice could learn and apply. Let them ask you questions and challenge you to explain the fundamentals. Some things you teach will flow easily, but others will stump you. Whenever you get stuck, take note of it. Your notes will help you pinpoint which parts of your craft you understand and where you have gaps in knowledge.

If you're capable of explaining the thought process behind your craft using simple language that means you deeply understand it. This technique is the reason creators need to share their knowledge with upcoming creators. If you can't clearly explain your craft, you don't grasp it well enough. Practicing exchanging knowledge effectively will deepen your understanding of the nuances of your art.

GIVE BACK TO THE CRAFT

What has your craft given you? Has it given you money or notoriety? Has it given you a solution to a tough problem? Has it given you the relief of expressing a feeling that had you speechless? Has it given you the escape you needed from the real world? Has it given you the map to your personal truth or a shift in perspective? Of all the things creativity has given you, the least you can do is give something back. Give a helping hand to a creator in need.

Key of Meditation

"In order to understand the dance one must be still. And in order to truly understand stillness one must dance. Without stillness, there can be no movement."—Eckhart Tolle

ALAN WATTS

There was a funny meme trending on social media that I can't stop thinking about. It's a green-screened video that starts off showing a boy panicking underwater. Then a text bubble pops up that says: "When you're drowning, but you remember you can drink water…" The boy stops panicking, pulls a straw out of his pocket, and drinks all the water. The video ends with an audio clip TikTokers use to jokingly seem wise. It's the voice of Alan Watts when he said, "A person who thinks all the time has nothing to think about except thoughts."

Alan Watts was a man of many interests. He went to school for theology, philosophy, and religion. He devoted his life to studying, observing, and applying many of the ideas and concepts that dealt the mind and soul. One of his core concepts was mindful meditation.

Before Alan Watts brought mindful meditation to the West, the word meditation conjured up images of reclusive yogis sitting cross-legged, deep in thought, utterly detached from the worldliness of life. Alan Watts smashed this concept and taught that meditation was a practice that could be done anywhere, at any time.

He made meditation accessible to the masses and translated the ancient practice into a modern context. He encouraged his students to meditate while they did household chores, while they went for their morning run, or when they were raking leaves and sweeping driveways.

Alan Watts embraced Buddhism but transcended all organized doctrines. He practiced many forms of meditation, and his teachings from his vast pool of experience have become a gift to society. His prolific writings and guided meditations are used globally by a new generation eager to escape the busyness of daily living and the anxieties that come with it.

THOUGHTS YOU HAVEN'T THOUGHT

Let's revisit the Alan Watts quote that trended on social media. "A person who thinks all the time has nothing to think about except thoughts." Even though kids and teens used this quote to make jokes about their deep thoughts, I dug deeper to understand what Alan was implying. Here's an excerpt from his full explanation:

"I remember when I was a boy, they had a common saying: 'Talking to yourself is the first sign of madness.' Now, obviously, if I talk all the time, I don't hear what anyone else has to say. And so, in exactly the same way, if I think all the time, that is to say, if I talk to myself all the time, I don't have anything to think about except thoughts. Therefore I am living entirely in the world of symbols, and I'm never in relationship with reality."

Think about it. When you meditate, your one goal is to clear your mind, to stop thinking thoughts. You seek silence. You're not just seeking audible silence. You're seeking complete mental silence. You're not thinking about the past or the future. You're letting go of all the ideas of the world. You're allocating all of your mental energy to focus on your present moment.

This is where you confront reality. In this headspace, your mind will make connections with the world around you that it's never made before. It's a natural psychedelic trip where you unlock the ability to think of ideas you would've overlooked in your everyday life. When you allow your mind to use thought patterns it has never used before, you will think of thoughts you've never thought before.

THE POWER OF LOOKING INWARD

All human DNA is 99.9% identical. In that 0.1% there's some information about our drug reactions, disease susceptibility, and a few minor physical traits. Other than that, we're all the same. Actually, did you know that it's impossible to determine a human's race from their DNA?[59] Race is an idea that turned into a social construct. Biologically, we're not so different. We're just 99.9% boring-ole-human.

The part of us that makes us the most unique is how our life experiences, our environment, and the ideas we've encountered along the way influence our perspective on reality. Your perspective on reality is what makes you unique. Your uniqueness needs to be explored. Hidden in the depths of your soul are untapped ideas, thoughts, and inspiration that can't be found elsewhere. The more time you spend using meditation to engage with your reality, the more effectively you will create art that speaks through it.

---

[59] Jarry, Jonathan . 2019. "McGill University." Office for Science and Society. August 18, 2019. https://www.mcgill.ca/oss/article/health-general-science/are-you-there-race-its-me-dna.

INTUITION

One of Alan Watts's main teachings about the link between meditation and creativity was that creativity was a deeply intuitive act and that meditation helped people tap into that intuition. One of his most famous stories is about his experience learning to play the piano. According to the story, his teacher slapped his knuckles when he made mistakes. Despite his best efforts, Watts struggled to learn the piano and became increasingly frustrated with his slow progress. This learning environment crushed his creative spirit.

However, a few years later, Watts had a transformative experience that changed his perspective on creativity. While listening to a jazz pianist improvise, Watts discovered that music was more than following strict rules and techniques but also about tapping into your intuition for creative expression.

He learned that creativity is not something you do; it's something you are. It's an act of creating something in the moment that's meant to be most appreciated in the moment. Inspired by this realization, Watts returned to the piano and began playing with a new sense of freedom and creativity.

He said the point of playing the piano is not the end of a song. "If that were so," he said, "the best conductors would be those who played fastest. And there would be composers who only wrote finales. People would go to a concert just to hear one crackling chord because that's the end." Alan Watts believed that the point of playing the piano was to simply play the piano. The value of creativity is found in the beauty in the moment of the act itself.

Meditation helps you connect with your in-the-moment intuition. The closer you come to creating through that vessel, the more creative you become. It's the transcendental journey of becoming one with your craft. The point of playing the piano is to play the piano. The point of dancing is to dance. The point of painting is to paint. The point of writing is to write. The point of being creative is to create.

Key of Completion

"The world is full of ideas, but to make an idea work, you have to see it through to completion."—Michael Dell

DEVIL ON YOUR SHOULDER

Every creator has a devil on their shoulder. In the book *The War of Art*, Steven Pressfield calls this force Resistance. It's the voice in your head that speaks with one goal in mind: to kill your creativity. It won't rest until you cut your creative process short. It tells you people will hate listening to your music, they'll laugh at your dance style, and they won't read your book. It exacerbates the imperfections in your art and tries to convince you that your flaws are the defining factor of your work. It makes you feel crazy for dropping out of college to pursue a business idea, acting gig, or apprenticeship while nobody else sees your vision.

This devil on your shoulder is the number one reason the world may never see some of the greatest creations ever made. His defeating whispers are your biggest threat in your creative process. It's understandable, though. He's offering the easy way out. Quitting is more convenient and more comforting than criticism from others, releasing a subpar product, iterating, and improving. It's safer to have a hard drive with your unreleased songs, a basement filled with your incomplete paintings, and a prototype of your invention collecting dust. That's where your comfort zone is.

There's a famous quote that says, "A comfort zone is a beautiful place, but nothing ever grows there." At the end of your life, when you're looking back on your journey as a creator, how do you think you'll feel? Will you pat yourself on the back for avoiding all of your potential failures, judgment, and imperfections? Or will you regret spending your life trapped in a cycle of self-sabotage, repeatedly conjuring up brilliant ideas, only to falter before seeing them through?

THE ONLY FEAR

That voice in your head is a universal struggle for all creators. Creative people are in a constant battle with their fears. For some, it's a fear of failure or rejection. For others, it's the fear of the unknown or being misunderstood. Here's the thing, creative geniuses only have one fear: unfulfilled potential.

The fear of unfulfilled potential is powerful because it trumps all other fears. Instead of having to overcome the other fears, it fights fire with fire. If you prioritize this fear over all others, it doesn't get rid of your other fears, but it does force you to make a choice. You either finish your work in the face of doubt, or you die unfulfilled. This fear should keep you up at night because the only way to fulfill your creative potential is by seeing your visions through to the end.

THE 20/60/20 RULE

Every creator started a project they know should see the light of day, yet they haven't touched it in months. Well, I have some good news. I'm going to share a three-step framework called The 20/60/20 Rule that you can use to see your projects through to the end. Each number represents the percentage distance you've gone in your creative journey, and each phase has a key phrase you can tell yourself when you hear those criticizing whispers in your head.

0% to 20% = "I'm just going to play around real quick."

Mark Zuckerberg once said, "Ideas don't come out fully formed, they only become clear as you work on them. You just have to get started. If I had to know everything about connecting people before I got started, I would've never built Facebook." The first 20% of your creative journey is when you need to start, but the voice in your head tells you you lack the time, inspiration, or skills. You combat this by telling yourself you're playing around. You're here to have fun. Nothing has to come from what you're doing. Jump straight into writing, drawing, or whatever the first step of your craft requires. The beautiful part about creativity is once you start, your mind gets lost in your creation, and soon enough, inspiration will find you.

20% to 80% = "Today, I'm not ___; I'm ___"

The middle 60% of your creative journey is when you have the idea for what you want to create, but what you have so far is different from your vision. You may be working on the first layer of a painting, the rough draft of a book, or free-styling bits and pieces of a poem. This phase is when the voice in your head feels threatened. It's going to say things like, "This is ugly. You suck. Start over." The best way to combat this is by concentrating on the task instead of the bigger picture. This will force you to focus on consistency instead of finishing. Tell yourself, "Today, I'm not painting a picture; I'm painting an eye. I'm not writing a book; I'm writing a paragraph. I'm not writing a poem; I'm writing the intro." These phrases will help ease your mind so that you can focus on the process.

80% to 100% = "I'm finishing this before ___."

The final 20% is when you're approaching the finish line. Maybe you need a few finishing touches, but for the most part, it's ready. That's not what the voice in your head is telling you, though. This phase is when the voice realizes that it has only one final move left to defeat you. It uses the fear of the unknown: Will people like it? Is it ready? How can it be better? These questions force you into a never-ending perfection loop. The best way to respond to this attack is by giving yourself a deadline. Say, "I'm finishing this in the next thirty days," and stick to it. It's also important to note that finishing, in this instance, goes hand in hand with sharing. Finishing your song means releasing it on all streaming platforms. Finishing your book means listing it on Amazon. Finishing your painting means sharing it on social media. Lee Unkrich, the director of Toy Story 3, is famously quoted saying, "We don't ever finish a film. I could keep on making it better. We're just forced to release it."

A TALE OF TWO CREATORS

Once upon a time, there were two artists, Jane and Nia, whose lives were magically connected. They were both born on the same day, had the same interest in art, and had the same skill level. They both thought the same thoughts and thus thought of the same artistic ideas. Jane shared her ideas with the village, and the people loved them. She explained them so well that the villagers grew excited at the possibilities of the ideas. Nia, on the other hand, created her ideas. She created them so well that the villagers hung her paintings in the castle, they erected her sculptures in the town square, and they sang her songs at their traditional gatherings. After decades flew by, as fate would have it, Jane and Nia passed away on the same day. Their tombstones read:

Jane: Here lies a great talker.
Nia: Here lies a great artist.
Completing your work or not is the difference between you taking

on the reputation of Jane or Nia—a life of unfulfilled potential or a life of creative impact. Choose your path.

* * *

Did any of these keys spark an interesting thought?
Share it with me at WorldOfCreatives.com

Key of Adaptability

"When you're finished changing, you're finished."—Benjamin Franklin

CHARLIE D'AMELIO

In 2007, a three-year-old named Charli D'Amelio turned her living room into her own personal dance stage. Recognizing her spark, her parents cultivated her artistry. For ten years, she trained in the rigor of competitive dance, solidifying fundamentals that would later transform her life.

In 2019, while dancers were still primarily focused on the traditional path to success, Charli saw an opportunity to leverage her skills and express herself in a new way. At the core of her strategy was one clear tactic: adaptability.

Around this time, TikTok shook the world. TikTok was a new social media app that was all about sharing short, creative videos. Their platform thrived on creating content around recent trends with popular background music. Charli's ability to quickly adapt to these changes, choreographing catchy dances to trending songs, made her stand out. She catapulted herself to stardom, amassing over 150 million followers in a few years. Her style of short, engaging, and rhythmic dance videos became a standard on TikTok. She went from riding trends to shaping them. She popularized several dance challenges, dance moves, and songs.

Charli's story shows how important it is for creators to be adaptable. By being open to new ideas and using them to be creative, Charli became the face of dance in a generation backed by digital entertainment.

ADAPT OR DIE

Adapt or die. That's the fundamental rule of nature. Charles Darwin hit it on the head when he said, "It is not the strongest or the most intelligent who will survive but those who can best manage change." While the concept is known for its application to surviving life, it also applies to the survival of your creativity. The creative process is full of surprises, so creative geniuses adapt in ways most people can't. Their fluidity is a superpower.

It touches every aspect of their life. On a small scale, it's how they react to mishaps during their creative process; a mistaken drop of paint on their canvas, an error in their code, or playing the wrong key on the piano. On a larger scale, it's how they navigate their ever-changing industries; the impact of A.I., a shift in fashion trends, or a new genre of music.

At the root of adaptability is optimism. Optimism convinces you there's a solution to every problem. It gives you hope there will always be a way to leverage incoming change. Most creators perceive these changes as a threat, but creative geniuses view them as an opportunity. When you teach yourself how to engage, learn, and adapt, you will thrive wherever the wind takes you. There's beauty in each season.

YOUNGER GENERATION

Have you ever felt misunderstood by the older generation? Do you complain about the younger generation? This dichotomy happens because each generation enters society and completely changes how we do things. Sometimes it's minor changes, but other times it completely shifts traditional ways of thinking. This leaves the older generation feeling disdain toward the younger ones. Their music sounds different. Their fashion feels nonsensical. Their movies lack substance. Their ideologies are outrageous.

An article written by the BBC compiled a list of the most common complaints about Millennials and compared them to records from the past.[60] They found that history repeats itself. Records dating back thousands of years revealed that humans have always criticized young people about similar things. The older generations, spanning centuries, always think the younger generation are lazy, self-obsessed, immature know-it-alls who are ruining religion and spending too much money. The truth is it's not solely a Gen X's view on Millennials. It's the natural order of the world. Millennials will think the same about Gen Z, Gen Z will have the same opinion about Gen Alpha, and history will continue cycling.

The uncomfortable truth is the world will change, and your foundational truths might change with it. The ideas and beliefs you were born into, the techniques you practiced to master your craft, and the information you learned in school are the cornerstones of your reality but they don't actually have permanence in the world around you. The world is constantly morphing, and you're only experiencing a

---

[60] Ruggeri, Amanda. 2017. "People Have Always Whinged about Young Adults. Here's Proof." Bbc.com. 2017. https://www.bbc.com/worklife/article/20171003-proof-th at-people-have-always-complained-about-young-adults.

snapshot of it changing. It will make you feel uneasy. You may attempt to do everything you can to hold onto the past, but, as the research showed, these changes and society's reactions to them are inevitable. Like Heraclitus once said, "Change is the only constant in life." It's the only guarantee.

CHANGE IS INEVITABLE

Each new generation of humans charters in a shift in creativity. Art, music, fashion, food, humor, entertainment, style, ideas, language, techniques, tools, technology, and other unpredictable factors all encompass the ever-changing creative world. The deeper you are in your craft, the sooner you will start to see these changes happening. These changes can flip a creative industry on its head, creating or killing careers, shifting the way money flows, or even retiring traditional techniques.

When designers began to transition to working on computers in the late 80s, they encountered a period of uncertainty. Up until then, design work was done by hand, using traditional tools like pencils, pens, and drafting tables. While some designers were excited about the new possibilities that computer tools offered, many were hesitant to embrace the latest technology.

But as time passed, the benefits of using computers in design became increasingly evident. Unfortunately, the designers who adapted slowly were left behind. It was too late for them to catch up to the early adopters who already mastered the new tools.

Designers like Jonathan Ive, the brilliant mind behind the iconic Apple products, Massimo Vignelli, one of the pioneers of digital design, and Philippe Starck, the celebrated French interior designer, are just a few examples of designers who successfully embraced the shift to digital and maintained their positions at the top of their field. These creators demonstrated that by adapting to the new technology, they could remain ahead of the curve and achieve greater success in their competitive industry.

We see it time and time again. When Charli D'Amelio noticed a new emerging platform, she didn't turn a blind eye to follow the formula of past dancers. She made a strategic decision to adapt to a new medium. She evolved with the trends.

The lesson here is that change is coming, so keep an eye out for it. When you see it coming, it may shock you but don't run. If it's a new technique, experiment with it. If it's a new idea, research it. If it's a new technology, test it. Confront change with a curious mind. Maya Angelou once said, "If you don't like something, change it. If you can't change it, change your attitude," so I'm not asking you to like it. But you do have to get close to it. Embrace it. Understand it.

BE THE CHANGE YOU SEE IN THE WORLD

"The measure of intelligence is the ability to change." This quote by Albert Einstein drives home the idea that creative geniuses are the ones who can anticipate and adjust to the shifts in their environment instead of getting left behind. They use their ability to adapt to become the influencers of each new wave, graduating from being changed by the world to changing the world. As the writer George Bernard Shaw once stated, "Progress is impossible without change, and those who cannot change their minds cannot change anything."

To become a leader of the new generation, identify and capitalize on these changes. Start by following the changes with a curious mind. Seek new opportunities for growth and innovation, even if they are outside your comfort zone. Once you master the latest tastes, tools, or techniques, push the industry forward by blending the old with the new to create novel but familiar experiences.

Key of Eternity

CREATIVE SPIRIT

Creativity is more than a skill or a talent; it's a powerful force that exists within all of us. When we create, we connect with our deepest selves and the world around us. When someone says, "You have a creative spirit," they're acknowledging the spiritual nature of creativity. Creators use it to navigate the landscape of their emotions, explore their boundless imagination, and express themselves. As author Deepak Chopra observed, "Creativity is the language of the soul. It is a way of expressing our deepest thoughts, feelings, and aspirations." This universal language is the voice of everything we create. It's how we speak things into existence. It's the knot that ties your mental, emotional, and physical body together to transform thoughts into reality.

IDEAS NEVER DIE

Ideas never die; they get replaced. They only get replaced when a worthy opposing idea comes and takes its place. The idea is always out there; we just never acknowledge it. So, ideas spread, they build on each other, they adapt, they combine, but they never die.

Even when an idea lays idle, no longer popular or relevant, it can still resurface and be relevant again at a later time. Once an idea is shared, it never truly dies completely. It continues to exist in some form or another, waiting to be rediscovered or reimagined by someone else. As William S. Burroughs once put it, "I have never seen an idea die. They just keep coming back." So, fight for your idea's life. Champion them in the face of opposition because your ideas can take on a life of its own in the minds of others.

A UNIT OF INFORMATION

The more information you have, the more connections you can make to inspire new ideas. That's why information shapes our understanding of the world around us. For centuries, human's quest for information has resulted in the innovations you see in the world around you, and yet there is still so much we don't know. It's mind-boggling to think about all the forgotten stories, erased history, and deliberately hidden ideas.

Take, for instance, the notebooks of Leonardo da Vinci, one of the greatest geniuses to ever live. He was a master artist, scientist, inventor, and visionary. His notebooks are packed with his ideas, sketches, and observations, covering a wide range of topics. Yet, only one-third of his notebooks are published, and, likely, there are still many more that have yet to be discovered.

In that small percentage of published work, we've read reality-shifting concepts ahead of his time. This means there may also be ideas in his other notebooks that could potentially alter the trajectory of humanity. His ideas and insights could inspire discoveries, new technologies, and new ways of thinking about the world. But unfortunately, much of this knowledge is hidden from us.

This raises a bigger question about the accessibility of knowledge in general. There are countless other examples of important information that is not widely available, whether because it's been lost to time, hidden away by those in power, or not deemed important enough to preserve. For example, many of the historical records of marginalized communities have been overlooked or erased, leaving groups of people misinformed about their past. Without knowing your history, it's difficult knowing who you are. As a society, we need to figure out how we can preserve and share information so that we can pull from it to solve our shared problems. Once the information is accessible, we can collaborate to potentially change our world for the better.

AN INFINITE BUCKET

Creativity comes from an infinite source. It's a bucket that keeps on giving. In the words of poetic genius Maya Angelou, "You can't use up creativity. The more you use, the more you have." The more you paint, sing, dance, or create anything, the more creative you become. It doesn't matter if you're nine years old or ninety. Your creativity will keep expanding the more you use it.

When you lean into creativity, one idea can have infinite adaptations. We see this demonstrated a lot in business. Businesses start as one thing and pivot to another, morphing to find their place in the world. YouTube was originally a video dating site, Twitter was a podcasting platform, and Netflix was a DVD rental-by-mail service. All of these businesses changed to become what they are today. The only way for them to remain a thriving business is to continuously tap into the infinite source of creativity to improve on their idea. If a business comes to a standstill, it will eventually die if it doesn't adapt.

Creativity is where you can always find inspiration. Even one source can trigger an infinite amount of inspiration. Love is a prime example. Love has been a source of creative inspiration for as long as humans have been creating art. This theme is in ancient texts and artifacts from many cultures, including ancient Egyptian's love poems, the Greek myth of Orpheus and Eurydice, and the Indian epic poem, the *Mahabharata*. To this day, we still pull from Love to create in novel ways.

Pour creativity's infinite bucket into your soul. The more you shower in its new ideas, inspiration, and personal growth, the more powerful you will become. Allow it to transform you and the way you create. Creativity is a supernatural force from within that yields marvelous, life-changing results. But it is up to you to activate and harness this force of nature.

Key of Branding

"Your personal brand is what people say about you when you're not in the room."—Jeff Bezos

THE UNCOMFORTABLE TRUTH ABOUT WHAT YOU'RE KNOWN FOR

The creators you admire have more to them than the boxes you place them in. There are more sides to Shakespeare than playwrights, Steve Jobs than technological innovations, and Walt Disney than Mickey Mouse. Often, these remarkable creative geniuses possess a wide range of skills, experiences, and passions that go beyond the realms of their most famous accomplishments. The deeper I researched their lives, the more multifaceted they became.

Unfortunately, they're not commonly known for their personal lives. They're known for their quotes, creations, and ideologies. These contributions encompass their personal brands. It's an uncomfortable truth creators face when going down their path to success. Their life and personality have so many facets, yet there are only a few things that people know them for. Most times, it's difficult even to count all the things they're known for on one hand.

Living with this fact is tough, but harnessing it can be helpful. If you know that everybody you meet will label you with three things, control what those things are. If you do this effectively, you will orchestrate a powerful personal brand.

CREATING A LASTING IMPRESSION IN A COMPETITIVE WORLD

In today's increasingly competitive world, establishing and maintaining a personal brand is more important than ever. Since every human is creative, every creative industry is saturated with creators trying to make a name for themselves. That's why you shouldn't try to be everything to everybody. Your brand is the culmination of all the core things you want to be known for that will help you stand out from the crowd.

A personal brand is a simple, concise way of communicating who you are and what you stand for, making it easier for others to recognize and remember you. At its core, your personal brand should be a single, powerful sentence that encapsulates your identity, your style, your target audience, and the message you want to convey.

What's the core sentence people say when they share your creations? It can't be a long list of things. You have to earn that by building a long-term relationship with your fans. At the beginning of your journey, it's best to choose a simplified identity that embodies who you are. What's your name? Is it your real name or an alias, because it shouldn't be both? What style of art, music, or dance do you create? If it's a unique style, name it. Who is your target audience? Don't say "everybody." Is it heartbroken teenage girls, or is it middle-aged men seeking motivation? Whoever it is, narrow it down to a clear group of people. What's the message you're sending to this group of people? Okay, now take your message, and tweak it until it's one powerful sentence. These answers will help you craft a simplified identity that accurately represents who you are and what you do.

There are a lot of creators who struggle to choose a personal brand because they hate being labeled. I understand why. As creators, we fear being put in a box because the limitations of a label feel unbreakable. We run from anything that has a chance of suppressing our creative spirit.

The difference between the typical label and a personal brand is that the latter is self-identified. Choosing your brand should feel empowering because you're choosing your label. You have the freedom to be whoever you want to be. Don't procrastinate solidifying your brand because, as a creator, people won't know who you are until you tell them who you are. Ultimately, your brand will serve as the foundation for your reputation, becoming the lasting idea of who you are in the minds of others. As marketing expert Jerry McLaughlin once said, "Your brand is a perception, and perception is reality."

IF ALL ELSE FAILS…

The biggest fear people have about leaning into a concrete personal brand is they believe they'll get trapped in one lane. I know there are a lot of aspects to your art, but you have to focus on one. Choose your identity and push it. Find safety in knowing that you can always reinvent yourself.

Kanye is a great example of the power of reinvention. Kanye started as a producer, then became a music artist, then a fashion designer, then a gospel artist, and along the way, he remained outspoken about his creative impact. Along his journey, some people loved him, and others hated him, but there's one thing for sure, Kanye remained a topic of conversation because he continued to reinvent himself at the highest level. He's a creative genius who leveraged the power of his personal brand to influence art, music, and fashion.

In an interview discussing the backlash he was facing entering the fashion industry, Kanye said, "A lot of people say, 'You have to do music.' I'm going to keep doing music, but what if people told me I couldn't rap? What would have happened? What if people told me I couldn't perform? You know, I'm only 36 years old. I have other goals and other things, and I'm going to use my platform, every platform, to stand up and say, 'I want to make something. I want to make the next Ralph Lauren.'"

Kanye knew that by staying true to himself, he could pursue any creative path. Throughout all of his transformations, he's remained confident and candid. He consistently preached the value of believing in yourself. That value was the anchor that allowed him to pivot to each industry while maintaining his fanbase.

The key here is that you can continuously reinvent yourself. If you're unhappy with your creative journey or inspired to pursue another path, don't view your personal brand as a roadblock. Your audience will understand your transition as long as you stay true to yourself while shining a light on your new passions.

Key of Confidence

"Believe you can, and you're halfway there."—Theodore Roosevelt

THE DREAMER'S CURSE

Have you ever woken up from an epic dream and tried to explain it to someone else? You probably stumbled on your words and forgot the nuances that made it great. Remembering the essence of a dream is easy, but sharing it with others is a challenging feat.

That's the dreamer's curse. Every creator dreams of what the world will look like if they implement their idea. The problem comes when they struggle trying to explain their dream to others. Other people's confusion often translates into doubt, disbelief, and negative criticism making the creator feel misunderstood and alone. Unfortunately, the only way for other people to see your dream the way you see it is to pursue it yourself. While publicly building your idea, people will eventually get a clearer picture of your vision.

Coco Chanel was a French fashion designer famous for revolutionizing women's fashion. Before her time, women's fashion was dominated by corsets, bustles, and other constrictive undergarments paired with layers of skirts and flashy hats and jewelry. Coco Chanel flipped everything on its head. Starting her career, she faced resistance from the fashion industry. Her minimalist designs were a stark contrast to the elaborate women's fashion trends at the time. Some critics dismissed her designs as too plain, while others said they lacked imagination. The designer Paul Poiret famously called her designs "unforgivable" and criticized her for copying men's fashion.

Chanel persevered. She continued to innovate. She rejected traditional designs, opting instead for simple lines and looser clothing, letting the body move freely. She used neutral colors and subtle touches, such as pearls and chains, to create a sense of elegance and sophistication. Coco Chanel went on to create some of the most iconic designs of the 20th century, and her dream for fashion continues to influence designers today.

Nobody is going to believe in you if you don't believe in yourself first. Your ideas are yours, nobody else's. So, proudly take ownership of them. Your belief in your dream is the fuel needed to bring it to life. If you don't believe in it, who will?

WE'RE ALL HUMAN

When we look at the massive marble sculpture of *David*, the hyper-realistic sci-fi movie *Avatar*, or technological advancements like artificial intelligence, it's easy to feel inadequate or inferior by the massiveness and complexity of those creations. Michelangelo, James Cameron, and Sam Altman seem to possess some innate, god-like creative ability to bring their ideas to life. But that's a false narrative you're telling yourself. Thelonious Monk wasn't born with extra fingers to play the piano, even though his music sounded like he was. Elon Musk doesn't have more hours in the day, even though his achievements seem like it. Johnny Depp isn't a shape-shifter, even though his acting roles look like it.

We compare ourselves to the most outstanding creators to walk this earth without acknowledging that they're human, too. They're humans who believed they could accomplish great things and dedicated their lives to bringing those dreams to life. They're no different from you and me. These creative geniuses put the time into their craft to become who they knew they could be. It doesn't matter your age, skill level, or background. In the words of Franklin D. Roosevelt, "The only limit to our realization of tomorrow will be our doubts of today." Greatness starts in your mind. Believe in your ability to change the world. Use the achievements of other humans you admire as evidence that you can do it, too.

THINK BIG

Lyricist J. Cole is such a proud advocate for dreaming big that he branded his record label Dreamville Records and his non-profit Dreamville Foundation. In an interview, he spoke on how creators should approach their dreams. He started by saying, "See yourself as high as you could possibly see yourself. Clarify and define your vision for yourself in the highest possible way that you can see it." He emphasizes the importance of dreaming big. He explains that you should set your vision so high that you feel "delusional." Right when you think you've reached the peak of how big your mind believes your vision could be, he said, "Push past that even a little bit." He follows up with step two: believe it and "do whatever you have to do to protect that belief." The creator you are destined to become is the dream you choose to pursue. So, define a dream so big that it scares you.

AFFIRM YOUR BELIEFS

You are what you think. Your thoughts shape your reality, and what you repeatedly tell yourself becomes your truth. That's why it's important to remind yourself daily to believe in yourself. When you intentionally practice positive self-talk, you can rewire your brain to cultivate unmatched confidence.

Write down your vision, quotes, and affirmations, and repeat them often. Drill these phrases in your mind. This will give you the motivation to push past everyday setbacks and follow through on the bigger picture. "It's the repetition of affirmations that leads to belief. And once that belief becomes a deep conviction, things begin to happen," as Muhammad Ali taught. You don't have to repeat them every day, but practice until your affirmations become second-nature thoughts. Lean into them to bounce back when you're feeling unmotivated. Eventually, these affirmations will become part of your inner dialogue, allowing you to instinctively face challenges with confidence and grace.

Here's my number one affirmation. Feel free to steal it if you're struggling to write your own:

I am a creative force. My ideas are valuable. I trust my intuition. I am confident in my ability to create novelty. I dare to take risks and explore uncharted territories; mentally, physically, emotionally, creatively, and spiritually. I believe in myself and my vision. I am excited to see where my ideas will take me.

A ZEST FOR LIFE

Believing in your creative dreams will unlock a joy like no other. You'll jump out of bed in the morning with enthusiasm, ready to mold the world as you see fit. Philosopher Osho once said, "To be creative means to be in love with life. You can be creative only if you love life enough that you want to enhance its beauty, you want to bring a little more music to it, a little more poetry to it, a little more dance to it."

Simply put, believing in yourself is fun. Even if you fail, your journey will be full of unforgettable experiences, meaningful relationships, and personal growth. When you believe in yourself, you pursue things that make life interesting. There's nothing more fulfilling than living with confidence, knowing that one day you're going to look back on your life, smiling cheek to cheek because you took a chance pursuing your dreams. Take the leap. Bet on yourself. Give it your all. And watch as your creative dreams unfold, filling your life with joy, passion, and purpose, leaving an indelible mark on this world.

* * *

Did any of these keys spark an interesting thought?
Share it with me at WorldOfCreatives.com

Key of Value

"Creativity is one of the last remaining legal ways of gaining an unfair advantage over the competition."—Ed McCabe

LOOP THOUGHT EXPERIMENT

Imagine if your entire life was an endless one-hour loop until you died.

What would you fill your hour with? Maybe you'd choose to eat a tasty sandwich, watch a short episode of your favorite show, and chat with your friend. Then it all repeats. You'd experience the same thing repeating every hour, 24 times every day. At first, you'll feel fine, but eventually, the sandwich will lose its luster, the show will be too predictable, and the conversation will bore you.

The lack of change will soon become mind-numbing, and you lose track of time in the repetitiveness of it all. After a few months, this loop will become your new normal, but you'll feel completely empty. You'll question the purpose of life. What started as an hour of enjoyment quickly turned into a life of misery. You'd give anything to take a key that would free you from this endless trap.

Let's bring this thought experiment to reality. The effect a looping *hour* has on you is the same effect a looping *day* has on you. Unfortunately, we live in a world where living the same day over and over is the norm. Wake up. Eat. Work. Eat. Work. Eat. Relax. Sleep. Repeat.

But that *is* the norm. It almost seems like your entire life has led up to this moment. You went to school, followed the rules, and passed those tests because that's what you were told you were supposed to do to become a contributing member of society. Then you reached the goal they told you to pursue. You moved into your new house, landed your dream job, and settled into a routine. The first few months of this lifestyle probably felt invigorating. I mean, you made it, right?

But over time, just like the effects of a looping hour, you get lost in the sameness of your days. You start to feel like you're operating on autopilot. You wake up at the same time as yesterday. You mindlessly drive to work. You interact with the same people. You eat one of the few meals you typically eat. You take a shower and get dressed for bed. Soon, the only thing that excites you is the novelty of the content you consume—news, streaming services, and social media feeds. This cycle makes you lose track of time. Multiple days blend into one. Then into weeks, then months, and, before you know it, years fly by. Eventually, you lose yourself.

Many of us are trapped in this endless loop. Some of us have been in it so long that we don't even notice it. "It's just life," we tell ourselves. Everyone around us is doing it, so it feels like the way of life. Nobody questions it. But for a second, ignore what everyone else is doing with their lives and ask yourself: I know I am alive, but am I really living?

If you yearn to break free from this cycle, I have a gift for you. It's a key that can unlock the days in your life, allowing them all to be novel.

That key is called creativity.

EVERYDAY CREATIVITY

When it comes to creativity, we often think of artists, musicians, or writers. However, drop your paint brushes, mics, and pens because creativity is not limited to those fields alone.

The Encyclopedia of Creativity by Mark A. Runco and Steven R. Pritzker covers a concept called Everyday Creativity that expands the standard definition of creativity to touch all aspects of our lives. Painting, building products, dancing, or singing don't classify Everyday Creativity. Instead, it's the creativity that flows through the originality of your day-to-day life. It's demonstrated in how you raise your kids, garden your plants, cook a meal, or even choose an outfit.

Everyday Creativity is typically undervalued and unnoticed, yet it's one of the most practical ways to exercise your creativity. Instead of reserving creative thinking to specific activities, you can apply it to your personal life, too.

THE DEMAND FOR CREATIVITY

According to a LinkedIn report, the number one soft skill employers look for is, you guessed it, creativity.[61] That's because, over the last couple of years, top companies have shifted their views on creativity. So why the change of heart?

As it turns out, creativity is the key to innovation in every industry. In a world where businesses have to innovate quickly or die in the dust of their competitors, collaborating with creative minds is the only way to survive. The ability to generate original, practical solutions

---

[61] Van Nuys, Amanda. 2019. "Upskill Your Employees with the Skills Companies Need Most in 2020." Www.linkedin.com. December 28, 2019. https://www.linkedin.com /business/learning/blog/learning-and-development/most-in-demand-skills-2020.

is a valuable skill. Companies are constantly looking for people who can help them stay ahead of their competition by delivering new and exciting products and services to their customers. That's why, in the workforce, creativity is crowned king of all soft skills.

UVP

Businesses look for creative employees because creativity is at the heart of all great companies. In 1984, Michael Lanning and Edward Michaels popularized a simple way for businesses to innovate constantly. The answer wasn't improving communication, teamwork, or problem-solving. It was more straightforward than that. They called their method Unique Value Proposition (UVP), the core part of a business that makes it different from its competitors and valuable to their customer. The best companies have a novel and useful UVP that helps them stand out in a crowded marketplace.

Tesla's UVP focuses on building cars that are sustainable and innovative. On their mission to "accelerate the world's transition to sustainable energy," they stand out by creating stylish, high-performing, but also environmentally friendly cars. Uber, the ride-sharing app, allows users to get from one destination to the next without relying on traditional public transportation. They prioritize convenience and flexibility as their UVP making it the best solution to a common problem. Apple focuses on sleek, simple design, Zappos focuses on customer service, and Airbnb focuses on unique travel experiences.

You won't find a billion-dollar company that doesn't provide unique value to its customers. Founders of these companies use their creativity to identify the core value they can offer. As the companies grow, the Founder's unique value proposition becomes the source of inspiration creative employees pull from to carry the torch. It's the

North Star the company uses to continue innovating even after the Founder moves on.

EUVP

In life, creators can gain an edge by incorporating unique value propositions into their life. This concept, which I call Everyday Unique Value Proposition (EUVP), involves taking an ordinary everyday task and intentionally making it extraordinary.

Consider cooking, for instance. Even though cooking is an everyday creative act, how can you add a twist? You can create a fancy cocktail with your meal, try to mimic a specific restaurant's recipe, or eat dinner for breakfast. You can combine different cuisines to create unique fusion dishes. Or how can this improve your relationship with your loved one? You could plan an unexpected or unconventional date, find unique ways to celebrate typically mundane milestones, or surprise them with a thoughtful gift on a random Tuesday. You can even apply EUVPs to any unremarkable tasks like trying to make different patterns on the carpet while vacuuming, folding your bedsheets into animal origami, or dancing to a music genre you don't usually listen to while you clean the house.

Decades ago, businesses discovered the key to success was prioritizing creativity. They learned that creativity was the ultimate creative advantage. The companies that adopted this strategy thrived, while the others withered away. While businesses use unique value propositions to win in their market, you can use unique value propositions to win in life. Look at your everyday tasks from unique angles. Challenge yourself to break free from your typical routine by adding a twist. Sprinkling unexpected elements throughout your schedule will transform mindless acts into memorable experiences. When you approach every aspect of your life with a spirit of creativity, you'll discover that beauty and novelty are all around you.

Key of Power

"An idea whose time has come is stronger than all the armies in the world."—Victor Hugo

POWER

Ideas are powerful. We cope with death based on our idea of the afterlife. We love people based on our idea of who they are. We spend ungodly amounts of money based on our idea of a brand. The influential nature of ideas gives creativity power. Creativity is the vehicle your mind uses to package and share your idea with the world. Every war we've ever fought, shift in humanity's eras, economic revolution, social justice movement, scientific breakthrough, and artistic trend can trace back to one idea someone had. They probably weren't the first to think of the idea, but they were the first to share the idea in a thought-provoking impactful way.

CREATE THE FUTURE

Chaos theory is a branch of mathematics that studies how things that start simple can become unpredictable and complicated. A known example of the chaos theory is the butterfly effect.[62] This effect states that a butterfly flapping its wings in one part of the world can cause a chain of events that leads to a storm happening somewhere else.

The chaos theory shows that seemingly simple systems can have unpredictable outcomes. It helps scientists understand things like weather patterns, an animal's behavior, and planetary movement. The world is a complex and interconnected place. Even the most minor things can make a huge difference.

Creativity spreads the same way. Tupac once said, "I'm not saying I'm going to rule the world or I'm going to change the world, but I guarantee that I will spark the brain that will change the world. And that's our job. It's to spark somebody else watching us." Your ideas have the power to change the world. Some ideas are more impactful than others, but everything you create will influence the trajectory of humanity. Each contribution has a ripple effect, influencing the next generation's ideas. Ideas have power and influence that transcends the limitations of time. Economist John Maynard Keynes suggests, "Ideas are immortal, and as such, they are the most powerful force in the universe." The future is impossible to predict, but instead of speculating about what could happen in the distant future, get out and create the future you wish to see. Participate in the creator's shared responsibility of shaping our destiny. The future belongs to the creators who create it.

CULTURAL GENOCIDE

The fairy tales, plays, songs, paintings, and other forms of art from the past give us a glimpse into who we once were. The artifacts we

---

[62] Wikipedia Contributors. 2019. "Butterfly Effect." Wikipedia. Wikimedia Foundation. March 4, 2019. https://en.wikipedia.org/wiki/Butterfly_effect.

investigate are all preserved art from the past. That means the art of today will become the artifacts of tomorrow. It's our footprint in the sand of human history that preserves the stories of our time. When you create something new, you're contributing to our story. Protect your creations to secure your place in the shared human consciousness.

Creativity is so powerful that destroying it is an act of warfare. This process is called cultural genocide. It's when an invader asserts dominance over the natives by demolishing their physical artifacts such as artwork, music, architecture, and literature, as well as the suppression of cultural practices, traditions, and languages. Art is the heart of a culture. Without it, the cultural ties that bind the natives together unravel, weakening them for generations to come. Once the invader strips the culture of its essence, they replace the art with their own and exploit or appropriate the resources they have left. They forcefully plant their ideologies in the native's minds knowing that one day, generations later, the natives will completely forget their cultural heritage.

In the late 19th century, Native Americans in the United States experienced a tragic example of cultural genocide. The U.S. government forcefully removed Native American children from their families and communities. They relocated them to boarding schools where they forbid their native languages and traditions, including banning traditional religious practices like the Sun Dance and the Ghost Dance.[63]

Here's some food for thought: Were any cultures stripped from your ancestors? If so, what ideas—tastes in music, religious beliefs, insecurities, perspectives on your community, etc.—were forced on

---

[63] "'Cultural Genocide' and Native American Children." 2014. Equal Justice Initiative. September 1, 2014. https://eji.org/news/history-racial-injustice-cultural-genocide/

them, passed down through generations, and adopted by you?

CREATIVITY IS CONTAGIOUS

Christopher Nolan's movie *Inception* is a mind-bending, thought-provoking thriller that explores the power of ideas and the intricate layers of the human mind through a team's mission to infiltrate someone's dream. Cobb, the main character played by Leonardo DiCaprio, spoke on the effect ideas have on our minds. He said, "What is the most resilient parasite? Bacteria? A virus? An intestinal worm? An idea. Resilient...highly contagious. Once an idea has taken hold of the brain, it's almost impossible to eradicate."

Inception's theme reigns true: creativity spreads like a virus. If an idea is remarkable, people will share it. Some ideas that cross your path will come and go, but a few will latch on your mind and cause a life-altering epiphany. This epiphany can be so powerful that you get completely lost in it, becoming your identity.

These ideas are transformative. Listening to a song could make you realize that external validation does not determine your worth. A painting could show you the power of embracing your true self, being vulnerable, and letting go of masks and societal expectations. While some ideas can be empowering, others can cause an identity crisis. For example, reading a book could make you question or abandon deeply held religious, philosophical, or ideological beliefs.

There are even ideas that adapt to your perspective of them. For example, a movie about the fleeting nature of life could pull you into a deep depression. On the contrary, someone else could watch the same film, and it prompts them to live more intentionally, appreciate the present moment, and prioritize what truly matters to them.

Ideas have the power to shape our world for better or for worse. Some ideas can lead to a medical innovation that saves millions of lives, while a military innovation could take a million lives. Some ideas address the urgent need to fix climate change and its potentially catastrophic effects on the planet and the future of humanity. Then there's Social Darwinism, an ideology that promoted the belief that certain groups of people were inherently superior to others. It fueled the rise of eugenics movements and provided a veil of pseudo-science to justify racial discrimination and oppression.

These examples are what make creativity a powerful and delicate responsibility. Your creations can shift who people are and influence them to act blindly in ways they never would've before. Ideas are powerful enough to shape our perceptions of reality. They have a profound influence on our thoughts, emotions, and actions. Like a parasite, ideas can become deeply ingrained and difficult to change. When an idea takes hold of your core, you share it all the time in your way of life. It spreads to your spouse, kids, and friends, and when a community accepts and shares an idea, it changes the direction of society. While Albert Einstein preached, "Creativity is contagious, pass it on," I'd say, "Creativity is contagious, pass it on with caution." It is crucial for creators to embrace ideas that promote love and bring us closer while rejecting those that perpetuate division and harm. By doing so, we can pave the way for a brighter future.

Key of Legacy

"Carve your name on hearts, not tombstones. A legacy is etched into the minds of others and the stories they share about you."—Shannon L. Alder

MJ'S LEGACY

Michael Jackson is arguably the most famous and influential singer, songwriter, and performer in the history of music. From childhood, he was obsessed with perfecting his craft. Michael Jackson created *Thriller*, the best-selling album of all time. His ability to make timeless music like *Billie Jean*, *Beat It*, and *Thriller* solidified his global stardom. Jackson blended pop, R&B, funk, and rock to develop a new universal sound. He used this distinctive voice to sing catchy lyrics and melodies. His stage presence gave his music life. He used groundbreaking visuals, flashy outfits, and jaw-dropping choreography to create unforgettable experiences. Medical staff stood watch at his shows because fans fainted at the sight of him.

We categorize Michael Jackson's legacy by the iconic moments he created. One of those moments was his performance of *Billie Jean* on the Motown 25th Anniversary TV special. It was the first time he introduced the world to his iconic white diamond-laced glove that became a cultural fashion statement. Also, during this performance,

Michael Jackson revolutionized dance by showcasing his new dance move, the moonwalk. The moonwalk seemed to defy the laws of physics. With every step forward, he smoothly moved backward.

Michael Jackson knew that everything he created was the cornerstone of his legacy. He once said, "Every day, create your history. Every path you take, you're leaving your legacy." That's why he valued challenging himself creatively in every aspect of his career. Instead of making basic music videos, he created compelling cinematic narratives. When you watch his *Thriller, Smooth Criminal,* or *Black or White* videos, he takes you along a captivating visual journey. Also, instead of performing standard dance moves, he invented his iconic signature moves, such as the robot, the anti-gravity lean, and, as I mentioned, the moonwalk. Each of these moments and creations became staples of pop culture. Even after passing away, Michael Jackson's artistic legacy continues to influence new generations of creators.

DON'T OBTAIN. CREATE.

Your legacy isn't built on the things you obtain, it's built on the things you create. The things you obtain are merely borrowed. After you pass away, the material possessions you own will be relinquished from your control and transferred to a new owner. On the other hand, your creations are the evidence you leave behind to let others know that you were here. No matter who owns it in the future, there's only one creator.

Entrepreneur Felix Dennis died with a net worth of over $750,000,000. In his old age he only had one regret. He said, "If I had my time again, knowing what I know today, I would dedicate myself to making just enough to live comfortably as quickly as I could, by the time I was 35. I would then cash out and retire to write poetry and plant trees." He learned later in life that creativity was the secret to fulfillment and building a legacy.

People rarely remember what you did, but they always remember how you made them feel. As we discussed in the Key of Sharing and the Key of Emotion, creativity is the most effective way to evoke hard-hitting emotions at scale. If you want to leave a legacy that's remembered for generations to come, create art so impactful that your audience can't help but think about it, talk about it, and remember it. Ask yourself: what are the most important things, other than children, you've brought into the world that would not exist without you? Your answer will give you insights into the legacy you're currently building.

WHO ARE YOU?

Who are you? The truth is you don't know who you are. You're not alone, though. Nobody knows who they are, and nobody ever will, but creativity is the key to understanding "you" more.

The creator's journey is a search for the "self." Dedicate your life to investigating who you are through the lens of creativity. Pursue this until your last breath. Even though there isn't an end goal, you will unravel fascinating discoveries about your soul along the way.

Find out more about yourself by losing yourself in creativity. That's the only way you will encounter unexpected facets of your being. Don't let the fact that you'll never truly find yourself discourage you from creating. Let it inspire you because there's an entire universe within you, waiting to be explored, with an infinite amount of worlds. The beautiful pieces of your soul that you take time to understand will become encapsulated in the creations you leave behind. As Henry Ward Beecher once said, "Every artist dips his brush in his own soul, and paints his own nature into his pictures." Art is a reflection of you, and when you create art, you're preserving yourself. The art you release into the world will be the ideas people hold onto as a memory of who you once were.

DON'T BE A "WHAT IF?"

Creativity builds legacies. Your most impactful creations are the breadcrumbs future humans will observe to catch a glimpse of your soul. These creations will continue to inspire people long after you're gone. You won't be here to see how the inspiration will take on a life of its own, but that's okay. Your responsibility as a creator is to donate your time, sweat, and tears to contribute to the ever-changing flow of inspiration.

Imagine a world where the creators you admire never created anything. What if Michael Jackson never performed, Michelangelo never sculpted, or Thomas Edison never invented? Usher, Justin Timberlake, Bruno Mars, Chris Brown, Beyoncé, Justin Bieber, and more of the world's most talented performing artists wouldn't have been able to be inspired by Michael Jackson's style, music, charisma, and dance. Damien Hirst wouldn't have been inspired by Michelangelo's exploration of the human body and mortality. This world may have never seen affordable rockets go to space, vacuum cleaners, and artificial intelligence because Thomas Edison would've never inspired Elon Musk, James Dyson, and Ray Kurzweil.

Let's take this thought experiment a step further. What if you don't complete that album you've been working on for years? What if you don't start that business idea lurking in the back of your mind? What if you don't finish writing the book you've lost the motivation for? What if you don't create a solo exhibition show of your art?

Don't let the world experience a reality where your legacy is non-existent. When you create in the face of adversity, you plant a seed that grows into a legacy that's fruitful with inspiration for other creators to pull from. As the great Michael Jackson famously stated,

"Consciousness expresses itself through creation. This world we live in is the dance of the creator. Dancers come and go in the twinkling of an eye, but the dance lives on."

Key of Rules

JACKSON POLLOCK

Jackson Pollock pioneered an art movement known as "action painting." He developed a technique called drip painting, where he poured and splattered paint onto large canvases, often laid on the floor. Although some may glance at Pollock's artwork and wonder why it fetches hundreds of millions of dollars, criticizing it as mere paint splatters, the essence of his creative brilliance requires a glimpse into the records of art history.

Art history began with humans drawing their observations on walls, capturing the world around them. Over time, our repertoire of drawing techniques expanded, and we invented various mediums to create more realistic art. Concepts such as perspective, proportion, and reflection aided in accurately depicting the world's essence on canvases. However, there came a turning point when artists like Monet defied conventional norms. Breaking free from the shackles of realism, Monet employed rough, expressive brushstrokes and vibrant, invigorating hues to portray landscapes, people, and other subjects. That's when technology threw the art world a curveball with the invention of the camera. The camera eliminated the need for art to look real. What's the point of posing for hours to get a realistic portrait painted when someone could just take a quicker even more realistic photo? In light of this, artists like Picasso challenged the status quo. He pondered, "What if I ignore the laws of perspective, leaving that to cameras, and instead paint a subject from multiple angles?". This sparked the birth of distorted art forms, expanding the horizons of artistic expression.

Here's when Jackson Pollock arrived. With audaciousness and unpredictability, Pollock posed a profound question: What if I create art that isn't of anything, free from any subject or representation? He discarded the idea of using any subject at all and, instead, painted paintings and nothing else. It only represented itself. This was the ultimate act of rebellion, not just against an art movement but against art history itself. That's what made him a genius.

Through relentless mastery of his craft, he defied conventional thinking and forged new techniques along the way. Do not be deceived by the seemingly simplistic nature of his paintings; his art is not easy to create. They required him to exert a painstaking amount of energy and emotion to create paintings so unique that they are nearly impossible to replicate. He created dynamic and spontaneous compositions emphasizing the physical act of painting itself. Pollock's novel techniques and the absence of a recognizable subject have had a lasting impact on contemporary art. Since then, artists have broken free from the chains of subjectivity, creating art for the sheer sake of creation, owing their liberation to Jackson Pollock.

LEARN THE RULES BEFORE YOU BREAK THEM

Even though Jackson Pollock is famous for developing a groundbreaking abstract style of art, many people don't know that he was proficient in painting realism. He received formal art training and mastered all the traditional techniques, just like all of his artsy peers. By perfecting the methods of the great artists before his time, Pollock elevated to creating art ahead of his time. He learned the fundamentals so that he could intelligently question them.

Creators of the past laid the fundamental groundwork to master your craft. If you go to art school, they're going to help you rewire how you see the world. At dance school, you'll learn how to cultivate strong body awareness and control. In film school, professors will stress the importance of framing and composition. By mastering the rules, you'll become proficient and knowledgeable in all the time-tested conventional techniques, frameworks, and traditions. However, to transcend conventional boundaries and explore new frontiers, you have to break those rules. This will unleash true artistic freedom, innovation, and creative thinking.

Don't rush this process by trying to break the rules prematurely. You'll only end up falling short of your true potential. If you break the wrong rules, nobody will notice you. If you follow all the rules, you'll blend in with all the other creators. Creative geniuses find a delicate balance between adhering to certain conventions and pushing boundaries to stand out. They don't break the rules for fun. They do it to push their industry forward. Master your craft so that you can confidently choose the rules you should bend, break, challenge, and redefine. Sometimes, if you masterfully break a rule, you can usher the world into a new era. Many creators make art; very few change it.

NORMATIVE AND DEVIANCE

In sociology, the concept of normative and deviance is the basis for whether a person conforms to their specific culture and the norms therein. Most people are normative. They are fine with following rules, whether formal or unwritten. They follow the status quo without thinking twice. But within each culture, there is a percentage that are the non-conformists, the rule-breakers, the so-called deviants. These deviants are usually outcasts because of their unconventional lifestyles, beliefs, or appearance. Sociologists study deviance to gain insights into the dynamics of social control. Deviant actions often lead to normative members of a society banning together to reinforce existing norms. Yet, sometimes deviance can challenge and reshape norms, potentially leading to positive social change and innovation.

NO RISK, NO REWARD

There's a common theme in the stories of creative geniuses who challenged the status quo to elevate their craft. Unpack the lives of Martha Graham, the mother of modern dance, Muhammad Ali, the most successful heavyweight boxer in history, or Thelonious Monk, the most influential jazz artist, and you'll unveil an unfortunate truth. Their efforts to challenge their industry were faced with doubters, people who outspokenly dragged their name through the dirt. In the dance, boxing, and jazz communities, those creators were deviants. They were the members who didn't want to conform. Like deviants in society, these creative geniuses became outcasts at one point. They were ridiculed until their creations drowned out the noise.

When Jackson Pollock deviated from traditional art styles, art critics questioned the skill required to create his abstract art. Some critics dismissed his art as mere "drips and drops" and believed that anyone could create similar art without needing true talent. However, over time, Pollock has been recognized and celebrated for his creative genius.

There's a famous story about Adam Sandler, the famous actor who charted his own lane by blending unconventional humor, relatable characters, and raw emotions. When he was attending NYU an acting professor took him out for a beer and kindly told him that he should reconsider pursuing acting because he didn't fit the mold. They advised he should choose another path. Years later, after he achieved meteoric success as a movie star, he went out with his friends and ran into the professor. He said, "Hello," shook his hand, looked at his friends and said, "This is the only professor who ever bought me a beer."

You will also experience the consequences of being a deviant in your creative community, but that's the risk you have to take to achieve your creative potential. The naysayers are usually your peers, creative professionals, and sometimes even your idols. Creators in your industry will struggle to understand and accept that the rules they thought were fundamental truths can evolve. Their core beliefs lack permanence. It's reality-shattering, so don't take offense. Respond with love. Instead, respectfully understand their perspective while holding tight to your truth. They don't hate you. They're resisting change. One day, as your creations take on a life of their own, they'll see the truth about creativity: Creativity evolves like everything else in the world. Dance changes. Art changes. Music changes. It all changes. You're pioneering that change. Like Albert Einstein once said, "The person who follows the crowd will usually go no further than the crowd. The person who walks alone is likely to find himself in places no one has ever been before."

Final Thoughts

"Creativity is one of the most magical aspects of the human experience. It weaves our dreams into reality, transforms mundane into extraordinary, and gives a voice to our souls."—Dwayne Walker

MJ'S LEGACY

Every human has fundamental needs. In 1943, psychologist Abraham Maslow proposed an idea that categorized human needs into five levels. Through researching his patients, he developed a theory rooted in the belief that people were motivated to meet their basic needs before pursuing higher, more complex levels of needs. He named this theory Maslow's Hierarchy of Needs, which has since become an influential theory in psychology.

Maslow's Hierarchy of Needs is often depicted as a pyramid because it visually and symbolically represents the idea of ascending levels of human needs, where each level serves as a foundation for the next.

The pyramid's base contains your most basic needs for survival; food, water, and shelter. These are known as your physiological needs. The next level above this fulfills our need for safety from impending danger. This includes employment, resources, and health.

As you move up the pyramid, your needs become increasingly

psychological and social. The middle layers include our need for love and belonging, like friendship, intimacy, and family. Then, right above that are your needs based on how your community perceives you. It's your need for respect, status, and recognition.

Lastly, we reach the peak of the pyramid, the highest level of Maslow's hierarchy of needs. This is the level very few people attain because they're trapped in a cycle of worrying about everything else. It's important because it represents the pinnacle of human motivation and achievement. Maslow called this level self-actualization, our innate human desire to reach our potential, achieve personal growth, and find meaning and purpose in life. Maslow argued that people who can achieve self-actualization experience greater levels of happiness, fulfillment, and well-being.

Maslow claimed one of the best paths to self-actualization was through creativity. He said, "Creativity is a characteristic given to all human beings at birth," and saw tapping into that creativity as a tool for self-expression and exploration. On our creative journey, he believed, is where we'd reach our full potential. Like Maslow once said, "Musicians must make music, artists must paint, poets must write if they are ultimately to be at peace with themselves. What human beings can be, they must be. They must be true to their own nature. This need we may call self-actualization."

The value of unleashing your creativity is not money, power, or fame, even though throughout this book I showed you it can attract those things. The true value of creativity is that it's a surefire path to self-reflection, self-love, and self-actualization. There's nothing more fulfilling. You earn a rare level of peace.

When you experience depth, understanding, and connection with a person, it translates into "love." When you experience that same level of depth, understanding, and connection with your craft, it translates into "passion." Find a person filled with passion, and you'll find a person enthusiastic about life. Their passion becomes their purpose. It's a fire deep in their soul that doesn't require anyone else's validation. The deeper they go inward, the more accurately they can express themselves. It's the ultimate form of self-love.

So follow your passion, stay true to your nature, and express your creativity. It's your path to experiencing a life filled with a strong sense of purpose and meaning. The clarity you gain in your values, beliefs, and goals will give your life direction. You will bask in life's blissfulness, embracing the beauty, truth, and goodness in it all.

Steve Jobs spoke at the Palo Alto High School graduation in June 1996 saying:

> "Make your avocation your vocation. Make what you love your work. The journey is the reward. People think that you've made it when you've gotten to the end of the rainbow and got the pot of gold. But they're wrong. The reward is in the crossing the rainbow…Think of your life as a rainbow arcing across the horizon of this world. You appear, have a chance to blaze in the sky, then you disappear. The two endpoints of everyone's rainbow are birth and death…Most people of your age have not thought about these events very much, and it's as if we shelter you from them, afraid that the thought of mortality will somehow wound you. For me it's the opposite: to know my arc will fall makes me want to blaze while I am in the sky. Not for others, but for myself, for the trail I know I am leaving."

This is a call to the creator within you. Most people are riding the rainbow of life, resisting the urge of their boundless potential. They're depriving the world of the opportunity to see them blaze in the sky. If that resonates with you, I promise it's not too late for you to choose to blaze in the sky. You're ready now.

When I started writing this book, I considered titling it "How to Become A Creative Genius." But after researching countless creative geniuses, studying creativity, and connecting the dots to write this book, I realized that title would've been a lie. Here's the truth: You are already a creative genius. You were born with the perfect ingredients. You don't become a creative genius. You unleash your creative genius.

Unlock the floodgates of the power of creativity and live a resoundingly novel life. A creative life is a life that pushes your personal boundaries. Pursue inspiration and expand your knowledge and experiences. Engage in experiments that reveal enlightening hidden parts of you. Each evolving step reveals the beauty in you, your craft, and the world. Craft ideas by making uncanny connections. Give birth to new realities through your passions. Bridge the gap between your imagination and the real world. Your creations will inspire people. It will change the world for generations to come. You will thrive.

The power of creativity is in you, anxiously waiting for you to experience it. So, unlock it and free yourself!

Go and feel deeply, express openly, create magically, and inspire limitlessly.

Go onward to change the world.

Go unleash your creative genius.

* * *

One last thing...
Did any of these keys spark an interesting thought?
If so, share it with me at WorldOfCreatives.com
Also, I will continue researching creativity and sharing insights there, too.
Stay Creative,
Dwayne